GH00992046

THE VIEW FROM THE LADIES TEES

TALES OF LOVE, LAUGHTER AND TEARS ON THE GOLF COURSE

To Anne,
Best wishes for
a very happy birthday
and years of happy golf
Peggy Strachan

PEGGY STRACHAN

Grosvenor House
Publishing Limited

Published by
Bloomfield Press
30 Bloomfield Terrace
London SW1W 8PQ
Email. bloomfieldpress@hotmail.co.uk
in conjunction with
Grosvenor House Publishing

Copyright
© Peggy Strachan, 2008
ISBN 978-1-906210-59-5

The right of Peggy Strachan to be identified as Author of this
work has been asserted by her in accordance with
the Copyright, Designs and Patents Act 1988

*All rights reserved. No part of this book may be reproduced or transmitted in
any form or by any means, electronic or mechanical, including photocopying,
recording or by any information storage and retrieval system,
without permission from the Publisher in writing.*

*This is a book for my father, because he
would have loved it that I love golf so much;
and for my husband, Ian, who is first, last and
always my best golfing companion*

TABLE OF CONTENTS

PREFACE

It was July, which to golf lovers means only one thing: The Open. In 1995 it took place at The Royal and Ancient Golf Club of St Andrews, known as the R&A or simply St Andrews. St Andrews is the home of golf. The name is a magical one, redolent of tradition, history and authority, and a round of golf on the Old Course is like the hajj, a must-do in the life of every passionate golfer.

I wasn't ready for a round yet. I'd taken up golf only a few months before, but I was thrilled to attend. For years I'd heard my father talk of St Andrews where he'd been an overseas member. Although he had only visited the course perhaps four times in his life, as a descendant of Scottish immigrants to America the connection was a vital one to him, a small yet significant component of his identity.

My husband, a Scot, and I were living in London and had been invited to join a corporate group at the event. As I circulated in the hospitality marquee, the room abuzz with the excitement of the wonderful afternoon in store, I had a sudden stab of longing to share it all with my father.

I asked permission to make an international call on the marquee telephone and, it being only 8.30 a.m. in Boston, reached him at home. 'Daddy, it's Peggy.' Pause. 'Peggy, well now, what are you calling about?' That sounds abrupt but for my father's gener-

1

ation an overseas call was something you made only when you had a good reason, and then you did your business fast and got off the phone. 'I'm at St Andrews,' I burst out. A pause, a throat clearing, another pause, then, 'You're at The Open?' he ventured, as if he had added two and two and thought the answer might be four. This was not right. I had expected something like: 'Gosh, Peg, that's just great! Did you see that wonderful approach shot by Tiger on the 4th?' or something of the sort.

Suddenly I felt guilty. Did he think I was showing off? Maybe he'd never had a chance to go to a major golf tournament. 'Yes, that's where I am. Are you watching it?' I asked. Another pause. 'Well, yes, I think your mother has it on.'

This conversation was turning out to be hard work, and very odd. I sent him my love and ended it quickly. Crestfallen, perplexed, I couldn't understand why my father didn't appear delighted, why he didn't tell me to be sure to watch his favourite players and to spend some time by the diabolical 17th hole, the 'Road Hole'.

But when I went to visit my parents in August I understood. My father's mind was beginning to slip away. Lewy body dementia, as we later learned it was, was invading his brain cells and within a couple of years he would no longer be able to tell his children apart. In the summer of 1995, however, the signs were still only barely perceptible and intermittent.

Nevertheless I understood right away that something very precious had slipped through my fingers. I had just taken up golf, my father's favourite sport. I had barely begun to play but was already addicted. And although I hadn't yet given them voice, somewhere in my mind's eye I had begun to nurture visions of playing rounds with my father, learning from his experience, delighting him with a well hit shot. Now these visions were dashed on the rocks of senile dementia. My timing was awful. I'd waited too long to come over to my father's turf; he was already walking off the field.

Just over three years later my father died of complications from his illness. His time wandering in the wilderness of mental confusion was mercifully brief. We held a small family ceremony at Mt

Auburn Cemetery in Cambridge, Massachusetts where we buried his ashes amongst my mother's family members. I didn't cry.

For weeks and months I didn't cry. For many years I had lived abroad, and therefore not seen my father often. However, even when I lived in New York City and my parents were in northern New Jersey, indeed even when I was a child living at home, a combination of busy lives and complex family dynamics hindered the development of a cosy and close relationship between my father and myself.

I was having trouble mourning him because I didn't really know him. I was having trouble missing him because, in my personal experience, there wasn't that much to miss: he hadn't played a big role in my life at any stage. But one day as I was driving to a competition at my golf club at, for me, the emotionally vulnerable hour of 7.00 a.m., my unspoken visions of playing golf with my father crept unbidden into my mind.

Suddenly I was overwhelmed by loss. Not just the loss of his company now and in the future; I was also utterly heartbroken with longing for all the times that we might have spent together over the previous nearly fifty years. And then at last I began to cry. I pulled over to the side of the motorway and cried out all my grief for my father, both as he was now, dead, and as he had been before, inaccessible to me. Then I pulled myself together, drove on to the club, and played my round for him.

THE 1ST HOLE
Getting Hooked

The View from the Ladies Tees is the story of how I learned to play golf. My road was long and winding and I often felt I'd been sent 'back to Start', for I am not a natural athlete and I was nearly fifty when I embarked on the journey. Never once, however, did I consider quitting. From the moment I hit my first decent shot, I fell completely under the spell of this glorious game.

This book will have most to offer to women who took up golf—or are thinking of taking it up—as an adult, especially for those, like myself, who were never especially gifted at sport. However, many of the experiences described in *The View from the Ladies Tees* will strike a chord with women golfers of all ages and abilities, and for the male of the species it just might offer some useful insights into the mind of the female golfer!

I come from a family of avid golfers, but I had never played it myself until I fell in love with the wrong man. Wrong or not, he was a man who loved golf. I began by walking around the course with him, playing a few holes and picking up my ball whenever I got in trouble. Tom had a lot of faults, but on the golf course he was great company.

The course we played was beautiful and we always seemed to have it to ourselves, even though we were only thirty minutes from downtown Manhattan. The seeds of my later addiction were planted and first flourished in that fertile Long Island soil.

In those days, however, I was a single mother supporting two children in New York City, so both time and money were insurmountable obstacles to my taking up the game. In fact, although I later married a Scot—they imbibe golfing with their mother's milk—I decided not to go near the game until I had unlimited time. I knew instinctively that golf was not for dabblers. Therefore, it wasn't until I stopped full-time work at age forty-nine that I took the plunge.

I grew up playing tennis. I had a million lessons when I was a child, played a lot then and afterwards, and was always mediocre. I froze at net, tensed up as the competition heated up and always ran out of breath.

The truth was, I hated getting sweaty, I detested having to dash around after the ball, and my hand-eye coordination—or rather the lack of it—prevented any advancement to the next level. If my brain managed to figure out a suitable strategy to out-fox the opposition, my body could not execute it. Frustration characterised nearly all of my experiences of the game.

The other disappointment in tennis is, what you see is what you get: a rectangle with a net, one—or three—companions but no time to talk to them, and fogged-up glasses. Not so with golf.

Before I took up golf, I had little idea what made the game so appealing. I thought it was a long, drawn-out walk back and forth over the same patch of ground, during which you used a skinny stick to hit a tiny hard ball into a little hole, and then you did it again, eighteen times! This activity took the better part of the day—including up to two hours of additional driving: the ones done in the car. Oh yes, and it also cost a lot of money. Well I was right about that part; little did I know just how much money. And that skinny stick? When you first try carrying all fourteen of them in a bulky golf bag, it's enough to make you yearn for your tennis racquet.

Here's what I didn't understand about the game:

- It is completely absorbing. The particular challenges of getting said tiny ball into that small hole can take your mind off whatever else ails you for a full four hours.
- It's a game you can play with friends of different ability. Because you are not trying to hit back a ball the other person has blasted at you, it doesn't matter if she, or he, is a lot better than you, or stronger, or faster or even smarter. The handicap system is the great leveller, and you can have a rousing match even with a far superior player.
- The ball doesn't move unless you make it move; it sits still until you are thoroughly ready to hit it. This means you can actually try to implement on the course what you've learned on the range.
- Golf is usually played in beautiful places. Even when you have not flown to some exotic outpost, you are by definition surrounded by green spaces, trees, birds, open sky and fresh air. But often you do fly off to someplace tropical and palmy—or even to blustery, windy, rainy Scotland with its marvellous courses, Ancient and new—and then the experience is sheer bliss. There are few more stunning sights in the world than green, undulating fairways leading to plunging, rocky cliffs and crashing surf. If golf is an addiction, then without a doubt the fact that you play it in some of nature's most dramatic settings is a big part of the fix.
- Mobile phones are not allowed on most golf courses or in the clubhouses. Need I say more? A quite typi-

cal and amusing sight, as you drive up to many golf courses, is the A-type, usually male, individual pacing around the car park with his mobile phone stuck in his ear, sorting out his latest deal.

- In golf you don't have to run (unless you left your pitching wedge on the previous green). Nevertheless you do get a lot of exercise. For those of us on osteoporosis-watch, golf offers four hours of brisk, weight-bearing walking. Golf may not be an overly aerobic sport—although the health books are forever recommending an energetic walk for the sake of your heart—but it beats the treadmill-cum-IPOD hands down as a pleasurable way to keep fit.

- Golf is a supremely sociable game. There is no chit-chatting between shots in a tennis match, but in golf you can and do. You might discuss the new chip shot the pro just taught you, or the pains you keep getting in your knees, or your daughter's new job, or how cross you are at your neighbour, or how the prime minister has got it wrong (again), or maybe even the best strategy for playing the hole. Whatever the topic, you can make the world a better place and still play the game.

Aren't these enough reasons to give the game a try? One goal of *The View from the Ladies Tees* is to give those of you who are just taking up the sport a few pointers on how to handle typical situations that you will probably encounter. Another is to share some of my own magic moments on the course, to illustrate the intense appeal of the game and all that accompanies it. What it will *not* try to do is offer advice on how to improve your swing. Not only is this best left to the professionals, but also, with a handicap still in the mid twenties, I am in no position to offer that kind of advice.

THE 2ᴺᴰ HOLE
Babes in the Woods

If you are just starting to play golf, do yourself some favours. What you are about to do is difficult, so you should do everything you can to make it a positive experience.

First of all, no matter how much you both want to, don't start out immediately playing with your husband, unless he is a beginner too. I have asked a lot of women who began playing golf in their middle years, 'What, for you, was the hardest part about taking up golf?' The answer I got over and over again was, 'I shouldn't have started by playing with my husband.'

Why not? It seems like the obvious thing to do. After all, that is probably one of your major reasons for taking up golf in the first place: to be able to play with your husband. Why not start immediately to share those Saturday afternoons on the links? With him, you won't feel as embarrassed, when you hit your early tentative shots, as you might with an outsider.

Well, unless your husband has exceptional patience, it just won't work. For him, everything to do with the sport has become second nature, and he will have no idea of the data overload you are dealing with.

He will start the round being supportive, but sooner or later he will revert to his own agenda, which is to shoot a better score than he did last week, and your needs will fade into oblivion. In an effort to hold up your end of things, you will start racing to keep up and your stress and anxiety will soon far outweigh any pleasure you might gain from the outing, let alone any improvement in your golf skills. On top of that his shots are so much longer than yours, even your best efforts look puny by comparison.

Far, far wiser to start out playing with another woman in a similar position or, alternatively, a more experienced one who can help you with tough situations and course etiquette. Play with her until you have broken 125 and are familiar with the basic rules. You will enjoy your time with your husband so much more if you are no longer such a babe in the woods—literally.

Did I just say break 125? You never hear golfers mention such scores. You hear newish golfers say how thrilled they are to have broken 100 for the first time, but 125? Surely nobody has scores that high. Well new golfers do, and more. When I started playing, I would regularly get a ten or eleven on a hole. My husband would invariably say to me, 'Just put it down as an eight,' if it was a par four, for example. His reasoning was sound: in calculating handicaps there is a cap on the score that gets counted for any given hole. However when I started out, I always put the full ten or eleven, even fourteen once. And I regularly got scores of 145 and over.

As a consequence, the day I first broke 125 was a red-letter day for me. After all, a twenty-stroke improvement is something to be proud of. If I had been consistently recording eights when I really scored twelves, I would have had no record of that improvement, and no obvious reason for some much needed jubilation. In fact, in my first year of golf I dated and saved every scorecard. In my darkest hours I would pull them out and take heart from my improvement over the months. That improvement was neither rapid nor steady, but the trend line was unmistakably in the right direction.

Another thing you should do when you start to play, in fact *whenever* you play, is to decide each time you go out what you want to achieve. Do you want to practice your game? Do you want to beat your girl friend, or your husband? Do you just want a little exercise and fresh air? Make up your mind, and play accordingly. If you really want to win, you might opt for a conservative but pretty reliable game plan. On the other hand, if you want to practice and/or improve your game, you could try some bolder, riskier shots. If it's windy and cold, maybe you just want to blow out the cobwebs and come home refreshed.

These are very different goals which call for different attitudes and behaviour. Then, if your game plan is not working, be flexible and change your goal. If you were hoping to improve your game but every shot is a shank, rather than drowning yourself in the lake on the 10th hole, change your objective. Enjoy the view and your friend's company and leave the golf practice for another day.

I think that beginner golfers could do themselves no end of good if they conquered the art of playing out of sand bunkers in their earliest days. I say this because I have seen, time and time again, beginner and middling women golfers who have such bunker paranoia that they plan their whole course strategy around the goal of not falling into any bunkers in the first place. This leads to them hitting their golf ball intentionally in the wrong direction, laying up short and safe instead of going for the green, and tensing up when they have to hit their approach shot over a bunker. Then whenever their ball does land in the sand, first they berate themselves for the failure of their strategy, and second they panic and can't get out. Women who are perfectly decent players in other respects talk themselves into bunker yips of the worst order, and the result is devastating to their game.

Therefore, I suggest that all new golfers find a good professional and work on their bunker exit strategies. These shots don't require huge strength or even amazing coordination. The shot is usually a short one and, although occasionally a little finesse is required, as often as not it is more a question of conviction (as in, DON'T QUIT halfway through your shot!). Learn how to get out of every conceivable shape of bunker, with sand of every known composition, and the course will hold few terrors for you—apart from the lakes, streams and rough!

Golf is a game where concentration is vital. One useful thing that new players can do is develop a routine which they follow each time they take a shot. Here's what I do: I take a practice swing from a position *behind* the ball. From there, I look out over the ball in the direction of play and choose a target. I point my club at the target, note the line relative to the ball position, walk smartly up to the ball and take my stance along this target line. I wiggle and waggle a bit, look out at my target a final time or two, and then take my swing.

Having a routine helps to transport you into a zone of concentration, much the way a mantra is used in meditation. It clears your mind and calms you down. And if you are religious about it, eventually your fellow players learn not to interrupt once you've begun your practice swing.

When you take up golf, be kind to yourself. For example, don't berate yourself because you don't get many pars. Remember that the par figures are determined for scratch golfers. You aren't a scratch golfer now and aren't likely to be one any time soon—and time may not be on your side. Instead, determine your 'personal par' for each hole. Let's say, if you are still pretty much a beginner, that it's a triple bogey on each hole. Then whenever you get a double bogey on a hole you deserve a pat on the back.

It is essential, too, to decide who you like to play with and under what circumstances, and stick to those conditions.

If you hate to compete, then don't sign up for the Club Championship.

Above all, don't let golf bring out the worst in you. You need to be able to go out on the course, bungle every shot, and forgive yourself by the time you reach the 19th hole. If you can't do that, then maybe golf isn't the game for you.

But if you can, then you can look forward to many years of enjoyment. Thanks to electric trolleys, golf buggies, caddies, and flexible golf clubs, many people play golf well into their eighties. It can be as much fun to play golf with your grandchildren as with your husband or best girl friend. In short, golf is a great enhancer of the golden years. Just try to stay out of the ponds!

THE 3RD HOLE
Training Your Husband

When I took up golf, my husband had seldom played golf with women. This is probably true of most men whose wives are not golfers. The men have played on weekends with their mates, or gone off on men-only golf jaunts, or played with their clients or their bankers. Women were not usually part of the equation.

So if you decide to take up golf and have dreams of beautiful and exotic golfing holidays with your darling husband and maybe another favourite couple, take my word for it, you will have to train your husband first—and probably your friend's husband too.

Here is what many men do on the golf course with women. They walk up behind you and noisily park their trolleys while you are hitting your drive. They talk or rummage in their golf bags when it is your turn to play. They give you unsolicited advice, both before and after you take your shot. They walk off the green before you've had a chance to putt and/or they 'give' you your putt even when it lies six feet from the pin. This may appear generous but really they haven't the patience to wait while you putt, plus in return they expect you to give them theirs at similar distances when they need it to win the hole.

While male golfers have a common tendency to grumble and criticise if the people in front appear to be playing too slowly, they are loath to let the faster group behind you play through, even when your group is a four-ball, the group behind is a two-ball, and your group has fallen behind. Rather than incur this, apparently, terrible blow to masculine pride they will hurry you up, rush their own shots—and mishit them—, get into a bad temper and generally do their best to turn a pleasant outing into a tension-filled race to the finish.

Another favourite habit of the men-folk goes like this: two couples go out for a friendly round enlivened by a little competition, perhaps between the couples or, often more amusing, the women against the men. By the second hole you discover that, in addition to the four-ball match you think you are competing in, the men have got their own private contest going, and you can guess which one takes precedence. All the jovial sparring and ribbing, the excitement of winning a hole, the energy and the attention are focused on the men's match and the women discover that they are just along for the ride, their contributions strictly irrelevant.

I am very lucky with my husband: he has never tried to give me advice. But most men cannot resist giving advice, not just to their wives but also to other people's wives and even to total strangers. I was completely shocked the first time a man I had never met before gave me advice. This was in the days when I used to practice at a local, public nine-hole course and I was often paired up by the starter with another player. I couldn't believe this man's cheek in presuming to suggest changes to my swing, after knowing me for fifteen minutes. It made me so mad that I couldn't hit another shot for the rest of the round. It prepared me, however, for the onslaught from the multitude of self-proclaimed pros who frequent the golf courses of the world.

These advice-giving men, though they might be excellent golfers, invariably have little idea how to teach or indeed *what* to teach in a particular case. Usually they offer a fairly standard bromide such as 'Keep your head down,' or 'Slow down on your backswing.' Or they say something guaranteed to ruin your swing for the rest of the week, like 'Your golf club makes a little loop at the top of the backswing. You should try to correct that.' A golf swing is a complex movement and although a man might correctly identify some wrong element in his wife's swing, it is probably a mere blemish she has developed to compensate for another, much more fundamental flaw, one which she is unlikely to fix in a single afternoon.

Some wives find this advice useful—perhaps because some husbands really do know what they are talking about—but most women I've met do not, and many become self-conscious and gradually fall apart. Husbands must be trained not to give advice unless requested, and even if you like your own husband's advice, please train him not to give advice to other women!

There are times, however, when you really could use some guidance, not about your technique but about the course—on the putting green for example. However a note of caution is in order here: be careful who you ask! Some people give fabulous putting advice, clear, concise and actually helpful. But others make a challenging situation hopeless.

Here's Simon's approach:

Me: *I'm having a hard time reading this green. Do you think this is an uphill or a downhill putt?* (Sounds elementary, but you'd be surprised how hard it can be to figure this out on subtle greens.)

Him: *It starts uphill, levels out, breaks a little right, goes downhill a bit, then ends level with a little break to the left.*

Me: *O.k., thanks, but that's too much information. Can you just tell me whether, in overall terms, my ball is above or below the hole?*

Him: *[silence]*

Me: *Pardon?*

Him: *Just take your putt.*

Mark's favourite trick goes like this: you have studied the green, assessed the situation, figured out your direction and speed, and programmed all this into your mental computer. You have also taken your practice stroke, settled into your stance and are poised to take your shot when Mark pipes up, 'Don't forget it's an uphill putt,' whereupon you overcompensate and hit the ball ten feet beyond the pin.

Alan, on the other hand, if you take your putt and misjudge by a few feet, announces without a nanosecond of hesitation that you pushed the ball instead of stroking it. Thank you, Alan. The fact that on that particular day you have consistently out-putted Alan hasn't stemmed the flow of commentary; indeed it might just have been the proximate cause.

My husband's own personal brand of bad habit is to fidget when I am trying to putt. He stands right behind the pin, shuffles his feet and shifts his weight back and forth. Or he wanders around the green, in and out of my field of vision, breaking my admittedly fragile concentration.

Training your husband is not easy. It is just exactly as difficult as it is to train him to do any other thing that would be helpful in life, like taking out the rubbish, remembering to call you if he is going to be late, or whatever other issue turns you into the proverbial nag. The golf course is as much a battleground as marriage is, and changed behaviour is just as hard to achieve.

The simple point is that all players are entitled to some basic courtesies on the course, and if the men are a bit sloppy about these when they play with their mates, that's no reason not to clean up their act when they are with the ladies.

Even the authorities agree on this: here are some verbatim quotes from *Rules of Golf* (R&A Rules Limited, 2007), Section 1 on Etiquette:

Introduction
This section provides guidelines on the manner in which the game of golf should be played. If they are followed, all players will gain maximum enjoyment from the game. The overriding principle is that consideration should be shown to others on the course at all times...

Consideration for Other Players
No Disturbance or Distraction. Players should always show consideration for other players on the course and should not disturb their play by moving, talking or making unnecessary noise... Players should not stand close to or directly behind the ball, or directly behind the hole, when a player is about to play.
On the Putting Green. On the putting green, players should not stand on another player's line of putt or, when he is making a stroke, cast a shadow over his line of putt. Players should remain on or close to the putting green until all other players in the group have holed out...

Conclusion
If players follow the guidelines in this section, it will make the game more enjoyable for everyone.

Truly, our golfing forefathers understood what this game is all about. I guess it took some Scots to have the sense to write it all down. You might want to keep a few copies of Appendix E, 'Helpful Hints to Husbands', in your golf bag so you can hand them out to your male partners if they start misbehaving on the golf course.

Notwithstanding their peccadilloes, men are marvellous golfing companions and, for me, a day on the course with my husband and another couple is golf as good as it gets. As the years pass and my husband's manners improve (and his progress has substantially outpaced that of my golf game), it just gets better and better.

THE 4ᵀᴴ HOLE
A Housewife's Work is Never Done

One of the difficulties in training husbands is the fact that men just don't understand what makes women tick. That's no surprise to anybody but how is it relevant on the golf course? The problem is the prevalence of a common but generally undiagnosed condition: Maternal Awareness Instinct Disorder (MAID). It is characterised by an excessive tendency to multi-focus and multi-task, and is brought on by years of caring for a household and its inmates. Here are some typical manifestations of MAID:

My husband will say to me, 'Have you seen my blue, long-sleeved jumper, the nice one you got me for Christmas last year?' And I'll answer, 'Yes, darling, I think it's on the back seat of your car where you left it after golf yesterday.' Which turns out to be where it is. 'Thank you,' he says, amazed. 'How on earth did you know that?' How did I know that? Years of practice noticing and remembering the location of stray gloves, schoolbooks, cricket bats, scraps of paper with important telephone numbers on them, and the like.

Or he will say to me, 'It's cold in the house. I think we should turn up the heat,' and I'll say, 'It'll warm up soon. The boiler just came on.' 'How do you know?' 'Because I heard it'

20

(we are two flights up from the basement). 'That's astonishing,' says he. No it isn't. Not after years of listening for babies crying, feverish children calling in the night, the scraping sound of chair-on-floor as my son pushes back from his desk fed up with doing his prep, the quiet click of the front door as my daughter creeps in late from a night on the town.

Is being a MAID a gift or a curse? I am not sure. It was useful when I was raising a family, but it turns out that this heightened sense of awareness is a major liability on the golf course. It is an affliction which rarely affects the men, for the things that distract me on the golf course are things my husband is blissfully unaware of. Sometimes, just to test that theory, I amuse myself by walking right up behind him while he is taking his shot, or noisily readjusting my golf bag when he is about to drive. He is oblivious to my antics.

Men of his generation have always had the luxury of devoting themselves totally to the project at hand, and they have developed the habit of becoming completely absorbed, to the exclusion of the outside world. It would take much more than merely his wife approaching him to distract such a man from anything, let alone his next golf shot. In fact, his wife approaching him is probably the thing *least* likely to distract him!

Most middle-aged women, on the other hand, have spent their entire adult lives practicing the art of knowing where their loved ones are at any given moment, and just what they are doing. When I took up golf, I had had those antennae up for twenty-five years. How was the simple act of swinging a golf club going to break this habit of a quarter century? And anyway, if it did, who would find my husband's jumper when he next mislaid it—which of course has begun happening with increasing frequency in recent years?

Little by little I have been able to persuade my husband of the merits of my argument: that years of honing my 'awareness' skills have taken their toll on my capacity for single-minded concentration, but that far from this being a defect that I should 'get over', on the contrary these skills are the very ones that helped me shepherd our children safely to adulthood. So now, whenever he noisily jams his golf club into his bag when I am about to drive, and he grumbles when I ask him to stop, I simply say 'Once a mother, always a mother', and he knows what I mean.

There is another aspect to the wife-and-mother thing, and it has to do with being a 'maid' with a small 'm'. Every one of us has spent untold hours cleaning up mess, usually the mess of others. Cleaning up mess is so excruciatingly boring that it leads to serious avoidance tactics: try to persuade your family not to make the mess in the first place.

On the golf course this heritage manifests itself in several ways. Take the question of divots. Most of the men golfers I know try to take a divot on their approach shots in order to put back-spin on the ball. After all, it's what the pros do. For many women, however, taking a divot goes against the habits of a lifetime, and after ten years of golf I still have an aversion to the practice. So strong is my reluctance to hit the ground, that for years I pulled my arms up as I swung through the ball, topping it every time.

My long suffering pro, Dave Wilkinson of London's Knightsbridge Golf School, has a very effective solution to this problem: simply tee up your golf ball *on the fairway* until you conquer the problem. Not allowed in competitions of course, but if you're playing that badly it's probably a good idea to give them a miss for a while. From time to time in the years since learning this trick I have resorted to it again, and it never fails me.

Here's another pitfall: women learn to do things efficiently. They put things 'on the stairs to go up' to avoid making unnecessary trips. They group their errands by location so as to finish them as fast as possible. And here is what many women do, at their peril, on the golf course: when their ball is in a bunker and the rake is rather far from their ball, they enter the bunker where the rake is lying and drag it behind them as they walk towards their ball, efficiently smoothing their footsteps as they go. The rake is then near to hand when they have taken their shot. Unfortunately, this constitutes 'testing the condition of the hazard' and incurs a two-stroke penalty. I know it saves time and steps, but the founding fathers of golf obviously never had to run a household.

Finally, one positive effect of all this tidying up is the automatic instinct to repair pitch marks on the green. I will not say that men don't do this. In fact they usually do. But many a woman cannot set foot on the green without casting an eagle eye around for the tiniest indentation in need of her ministrations. The fact that this behaviour might simply be evidence of a housewifely obsessive/compulsive disorder isn't important. It's beneficial for the course. So by the way, just in case you aren't sure about it, the technique for repairing a pitch mark can be found in Appendix F.

The 5TH Hole
Blue is the New Black

When you take up golf, the single most important decision you will make is whether your golfing wardrobe will be built around blue or black! You don't believe me? Then prepare yourself to own two completely different sets of outfits for the game, and to handle complex issues of colour coordination when you're only half awake.

There is without doubt nothing more jarring to one's aesthetic sensibilities than a woman golfer wearing a nicely tailored pair of black and white checked trousers with navy blue golf shoes, when a pair of black and white shoes, or even some smart black and tan shoes, would finish off the outfit to a tee. Conversely those chic black and tan shoes are an eyesore when worn with a trim pair of blue shorts.

When I first started grown-up work (after seven years confined to barracks with the children and the Hoover), I was very excited to have the excuse to dress nicely every day. I went straight out and bought the staples of my new wardrobe, two much coveted pairs of Bruno Magli shoes, one black and one brown. These were the most expensive things I had ever bought myself and I hadn't even banked my first pay cheque.

Big mistake, I quickly learned. Sure I was shod for any colour suit I might care to buy (once I could afford any at all), but I quickly figured out that I also needed both black and brown belts, black and brown handbags, black and brown gloves, and the sorry truth was that I never looked very good in brown anyway. Before too long I settled into comfortable monogamy with black.

On the golf course I have opted for blue. I have waterproof shoes in navy blue for winter, lightweight light blue shoes for golfing in Spain, gorgeous two-tone blue shoes for English spring. Everything follows from that. With them I can wear all shades of blue, most other colours whether pastel or bright, white of course, but neither black nor brown. Never black or brown! I once won the most practical and nicely tailored, lightweight windbreaker with zip-off sleeves at an invitational tournament. It is a splendid garment but it is black, so it hangs in my closet neglected.

When you are dressing for golf, it's o.k. to dress to show yourself off to your best. Why on earth not? We play golf at least partly to keep fit, ergo, we probably look pretty good. Why hide it? Don't wear baggy pants; these are the height of frock-horror. Nicely tailored bum-hugging ones are a must. In what other daytime activity do you routinely turn your back to the assembled company, stick your bottom out and wiggle it around, and not be arrested for indecent behaviour? What a chance—all above board—to strut your stuff.

I sat in a group of six golfers recently, both men and women, and somehow we got on to the topic of some men's dismissive treatment of women on the golf course. One guy said, 'These days no doubt we'll all be accused of sexual harassment.' 'No,' I said, 'what you're describing is not *sexual* harassment, just harassment plain and simple. It would be *sexual* harassment if you said to a woman, "I really love to watch you wiggle your ass when you're getting ready to drive."' Instantly Judy, sitting to my left and just turned fifty, piped up, 'Then I really *wish* somebody would sexually harass *me* on the golf course.'

Sadly some of us are now past the era of wolf whistles. When we used to get them we hated it; now a whistle or two wouldn't go amiss. So dress for it. But pick your colours well.

Clubs have a lot of rules about golfing attire. This is bad news and good news. In many clubs men cannot wear shorts unless they are also wearing knee-high socks. Perish the thought that we might see their calves. My golfing friend, Margaret, who lived for several years in America, told me that her club in Texas had a rule that a woman's shorts could not stop more than six inches above the ground when she was kneeling. What? Who measures this I want to know. Is it one of the duties of the head pro that he has to make each woman golfer kneel down in front of him while he presses a ruler to her thigh, so he can see if her shorts are long enough? And does this task make him the luckiest man alive or the unluckiest? In Margaret's view, the only relevant criterion for shorts length should be the quality of the legs wearing them. I agree with her, provided it doesn't get codified in the club rules.

Generally speaking, and not surprisingly, it is the more puritanical countries that are the strictest, but by that I don't mean Islamic countries, I mean Britain (remember the calves—that's short for Calvinist) and America. Catholic countries seem to be much more relaxed about, for example, the length of a woman's shorts, and it is common to see women golfing in short shorts all around the Mediterranean.

The word to the wise, if you are going to a new club, is to err on the side of conservative. Otherwise you might be forced into an emergency purchase in the pro shop and will probably end up with something you hate (or something black). The good news is that you never, except on some public courses, see people in t-shirts, blue jeans, cut-offs, undershirts or, god forbid, no shirt at all. It is a welcome change from what graces many of our streets much of the time.

One other tip: don't change into your golf shoes in the car park unless you are sure it's o.k! Really. Many clubs have a strict rule against this. They must know something about feet that I don't know.

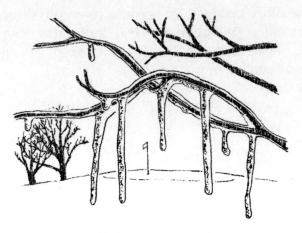

The 6th Hole
A Game For All Seasons

American friends often ask me what is my favourite thing about living in England, and I always say it is the weather. They think I am crazy, but the weather in England has improved markedly in the twenty years I have lived here: less rain, less fog, more sun. The more important point, however, is that since I took up golf, I think about the weather in a wholly different way.

Unlike my New England friends, whose golf courses for the most part pack it in around October and don't open again until April, here in old England, where snow is reasonably rare and even January offers many warmish days, we play right through the winter, and only the vilest weather will keep us off the course.

There are a few caveats. First, you have to layer your clothes as if you were skiing. When the thermometer registers close to zero, I wear silk long underwear—tops and bottoms—a cashmere rollneck pullover, another woolly jumper on top of that, then a fleece vest and finally a wind-breaker if necessary. I put on waterproof shoes, warm socks, wind pants over my trousers, and one of my fetching selection of woolly berets (better than ski hats as they don't crush the hair). In my golf bag I pack a pair of outer mittens to wear between shots and a supply of disposable hand warmers to stick in them.

Second, you have to tee off by 10.00 a.m., especially if the day is grey, because the light starts going after 2.00 p.m. The flip side of this is that in June and July you can tee off as late as 6.00 p.m. and still get in eighteen holes before dark.

One January morning a few years ago, I arose at 6.30 a.m. to head out to my golf club. I had committed to play in a Ladies Day competition, and even though it was dark and the temperature well below zero, the code of conduct is clear: if you sign up, you show up. My tee time was at 8.30 and I had a fifty-five minute drive ahead of me. In order to beat the rush-hour traffic I really had to get out of London by 7.15, well before anybody would have arrived in the pro shop who could tell me if the course was even going to open on that icy, wintry day.

When I arrived at the club, the place was virtually empty. Notwithstanding the reputation of the English for enduring hardship, on that particular day it seemed that most of the women had put a toe out the front door and then crawled back to bed. The only people there were Gillian, who had also signed up to play, and one sleepy staff member in the pro shop. Gillian and I looked at each other, shrugged our shoulders, and agreed that having taken the trouble to come here we were going to play. The staff member said that not only was the course open but also—amazingly—the regular greens were in use.

Gillian was without a doubt the scariest member of the club. She was quiet and aloof, absolutely beautiful, elegant, and immaculately turned out even in winter golfing attire. Her hair was always perfectly coiffed and she wore seriously good jewellery to the course. I could never decide whether she was a phoney or whether, in reality, I wanted to be just like her (or both). What I did know was that she intimidated me because underneath her un-cracked surface, she was a crack golfer, with a handicap of six. Mine at the time was thirty-two.

So here goes nothing, I thought, as we stood up on the tee. Just then the sun burst out and the whole course, the fairways and the trees alongside, all covered in a layer of frost, began to sparkle. The magic of the setting infected us both and we were in a merry mood as Gillian took her drive. And then the most amazing thing happened. Her ball, which probably carried 170 yards anyway, hit the frozen ground and bounced about forty feet high and forward. On its next bounce it again carried thirty feet, and so on until it was within a small pitch shot to the green.

The two of us looked at each other and collapsed with laughter. I hit my drive and the same thing happened, though I guess I probably still had an eight-iron to the green. We walked up the fairway together to my ball, the sky and our dispositions equally sunny. I took my shot. Perfectly judged, for once, it bounced just short of the green, then bounced again on the green, then bounced off the back of the green and sailed off into the woods. Again we dissolved in laughter. These conditions were clearly going to require a little ingenuity.

Gillian, therefore, instead of hitting one of her lovely textbook pitch shots, rolled the ball up on the green, but her rolling ball could no more stop than my bouncing one. By this time we were in hysterics. We carried on, trying different techniques, inventing names for our new shots while jumping around to keep warm, for about eight holes, then packed it in and went for a coffee.

I will never forget that day of golf in our own private winter wonderland. The trees sparkled, the snow shone with reflected sunlight, but nothing on the course could compete with Gillian's two-carat diamond ear studs.

THE 7TH HOLE
A Pain in the Neck

Golf may not require running, lunging and leaping, and it is not a contact sport (unless you count taking divots), but the high-speed rotation of the swing is very taxing on middle-aged joints and muscles. In fact as we age, just leaning down to get the ball out of the cup becomes increasingly difficult!

Since taking up golf I have had many pains, not just in my neck but also in my back, shoulders, elbows, thighs, bum and hips. Sometimes it's simply a muscle, complaining because it's not really strong enough to do what I'm asking of it. Sometimes it's a tendon or a bursa or a joint, grumpy because it would rather retire and become a couch potato than contort itself for my satisfaction.

So I have become a generous supporter of the medical and alternative medicine communities, and have helped fund the pensions of practitioners whose profession I hadn't even heard of ten years ago: osteopaths, orthopaedic radiologists, rheumatologists. If I could dispense with X-rays, CAT scans and ultra sound, I could probably solve the problem of global warming single-handed, but I might bankrupt the pharmaceutical industry if I weaned myself completely from anti-inflammatories, cortisone and muscle rubs.

I may have more Achilles heels than many of my golfing mates (and certainly more than Achilles had), but sooner or later they have all developed something that cramps their style. Ours are no longer young bodies, and golf requires a lot from them.

After years of looking for answers, I finally found the simplest one of all. I consulted a physiotherapist who explained that although I was generally fit, my major muscles were not strong enough to handle the strain of several rounds of golf a week. He prescribed a series of very specific isometric exercises to strengthen the muscles of my bum, stomach and thighs, trained me to do them exactly right, checked my technique each time I showed up for more of his pummelling and kneading, and shamed me if I hadn't been diligent. Without any doubt, this regime helped take the strain off my lower back and hips.

Motivated by the improvement, I consulted a specialist sports physiotherapist and, with his help, changed my whole approach to the problem. I finally understood that if I wanted to improve my golf game, and if I wanted to keep playing several times a week, I would have to take responsibility for my own body and not depend on palliative treatments. Chris designed an extensive programme of strengthening, stretching and, very important in my case, balance exercises, and increased the difficulty of the exercises as I got stronger and more flexible.

These exercises are gradually making me the master of my body instead of the reverse. They required a considerable investment in time at the outset, but they've paid off not only in many hours of pain-free golf but also in longer and better-controlled shots, and a lower handicap. I wish I had thought to go this route from the start and I highly recommend consulting a qualified sports physiotherapist early in your golfing career, before your aches become a pain in the neck.

I am also pretty scrupulous about warming up a bit before I start to play. Even if I don't have time to hit a few balls on the range, even if I only have three or four minutes before my turn to tee off, I go through a little combo aerobics/tai-chi warm-up routine to loosen my muscles and get the blood flowing, and then I do a few stretches. I take two Advil or aspirin, both before playing and after. I drink plenty of water during the round, I surreptitiously stretch out my lower back often on the way around the course and I do a few stretches at the end. Whenever possible I take a quick hot shower before sitting down to a long chatty lunch, and on the drive home I put my seat warmer on in the car. And if your car doesn't have a seat warmer, I suggest you trade it in for a model that does!

Why don't more golf clubs have a small gym or at least a stretching room to permit, indeed encourage, players to warm up before and stretch out after they play? Maybe now that the pros are paying more attention to this, clubs will start to install them. Meanwhile, however, old attitudes persist. It has been my experience that if you so much as stretch your legs as you prepare to tee off, somebody will comment (with a hint of scorn) about how 'good' you are to do that, or will remark (with a generous helping of scorn) 'what do you think this is here? A gym?' But to stand up on the tee in your cold, old body and fling a skinny stick at a tiny ball with all your strength, without any warm up at all, is surely lunacy.

I have always wondered who invented that weird thing men do, and call it warming up. They put a golf club behind their back, parallel to the ground, hold it in place with the insides of their elbows, and twist left and right three or four times. This ineffectual motion is considered an acceptable preparation, almost a badge of belonging, in the same way that so many tennis pros took up the habit of blowing on their hand before grabbing hold of their racquet in preparation for the next point. So I assume that somewhere in the collective memory of golf there is a Jimmy Connors figure who invented this golf club manoeuvre. I'd like to meet him and set him straight!

THE 8TH HOLE
The Anguish of the Un-Athletic

I have been playing golf for just over ten years, but it was only about a year ago that I finally discovered the key to the game for the athletically-challenged middle-aged woman.

Clench your bum!

Yes, really. The *gluteus maximus* is the biggest muscle in our bodies. Put it to work and it solves a multitude of problems. Actually, this is not rocket science, but I've never met a pro who even hinted that the condition of the client's raw material (her bottom, in particular) was relevant to how she might hit her golf shot. Too sensitive these days, I guess.

For years I played golf as if my club were the pendulum in a longcase clock. Look around you at the golf club and you will see that this is a common pattern among many women beginners who were not hockey stars in their youth.

On the backswing, their club arcs gracefully up, pulling the arms, the shoulders and indeed the whole body to the side and up, straightening the legs in the process. At the top of the arc, the club, arms and body reverse direction all at the same time, and swing down together, all of a piece, through the ball (when it works) and then up the other side in the same rhythm.

There is no leverage in this swaying swing. There is no extra club-head speed, there is no coiling of energy at the top of the backswing. The swing is neither efficient nor very effective, but it feels reasonably natural and for many of us it is the only way we can conceive of playing golf when we start out in the sport. Anything else feels so unfamiliar we simply cannot make it work. 'Agricultural' my pro called this swing, and I always imagined myself with a scythe, harvesting wheat in a medieval field—in Provence of course.

There are only two possible options if this is your style of shot. Either accept the fact that you will never get much distance, or else increase your power by increasing your sway and play havoc with your back and hips. The latter is the route I chose, and after five years of increasing pain and mounting physiotherapy bills, I begged my pro to help me find a solution. 'It's easy,' he said, 'just cut out the swaying. But you'll have to completely relearn your swing. Count on it taking you six months.'

If only! How about four years? For four long years I struggled to find a swing that felt like it made sense. I became obsessed by the position of my hands, elbows, knees and hips in each frame of the swing. I slowed it down to the point of paralysis, tried focusing on only one thing at a time, played only with my irons, played only with my woods, began teeing up the ball on the fairway again. Nothing worked.

I had lessons and picked up pointers, but the fundamental ownership of my own golf swing eluded me. I knew what each bit of my body was supposed to do. When I missed a shot I had a pretty good idea which part of me was misbehaving, but harness my whole body into an athletic instrument? This I could not do. I spent the whole time trying to put my body into this position or that, rather than using the power of my muscles to get coil, spring and leverage.

I recently found in my Palm Pilot some notes I made at the range one day when I was trying to distil into a few short instructions the key things I was supposed to remember about each shot. They look like this:

STOP AT TOP TOP TOP! If not, maybe not staying level. SLOW BACKSWING. THROW R. ARM DOWN & OUT.
Woods: Knees. Slow. MUST STOP AT TOP!
Driver: Knees. Slow & go all the way. Bounce off the top of backswing w. extended arm & body.
Irons: SHOULDER TURN BUT KEEP LEVEL. RIGHT HAND AND RIGHT FOOT TOO

This is a sport? It sounds more like a ceremonial ritual.

One day, in a fit of extreme frustration, I concluded that I was going about the thing all wrong. While my previous 'agricultural' swing might have been hard on my body, it had nevertheless captured something of the essence of a projectile endeavour. In those days I regularly hit my drive 200 yards; since abandoning that swing it had never exceeded 165. I realised that I was much too hung up on the details of the swing, the slo-mo frames, when what I really needed was to let my body talk. So I put my mind onto figuring out how the body turns itself into, in effect, a catapult.

I've watched a lot of professional golfers, both live and on television. That is an excellent way to get a sense of the rhythm of the golf swing, but you can't figure out anything about how the golfer uses his body to produce that swing. The whole movement happens too fast and looks so easy. Then one magic day my love for another sport, a very American one, led me to a revelation.

I love to watch American baseball. Maybe this is because going to New York Yankees games was something I *did* do with my father. My mother, from Boston, remained a die-hard Red Sox fan so he recruited fellow Yankee fans from among his children. He taught me the rules, educated me in baseball strategy and infused me with his passion for the game and his home team. I still find few things more enjoyable than an afternoon in the ball park, eating hot dogs and following the ebb and flow of excitement that are typical of that sport.

In particular I love to watch how different batters stand up to the pitcher, and I am fascinated by the way they ready themselves for the pitch. Since the ball will come at them so fast, they have to take their bat back ahead of time. Unlike in golf, therefore, the observer has ample time to see what the player looks like in that moment before he releases his swing.

A batter at the ready holds his bat way out behind and up high. His weight is almost entirely on his back foot, and many batters lift their front foot off the ground repeatedly, ready to spring. As I was watching a game one day, I realised that this foot-lifting was telling me something vital: that the muscles of the batter's lower body were fully engaged, else how could he keep lifting that foot without falling over. The muscles in his bum, thighs and calves were all working overtime in order, first, to balance him in the ready position until the ball came flying at him, and then to permit him to firmly plant his front foot and twist his hips forward as his arms arced through the swing. This, I thought, is what I must somehow capture.

Then, oddly, another image came to mind. I was once blessed with the opportunity to observe an operatic master class led by that splendid baritone, Thomas Hampson. I was intrigued by his session with one aspiring singer, in which he coaxed the young man to convert his lower body, from his hips down, into a stable pedestal on which his upper body floated, giving him complete freedom to open his lungs and heart to musical expression. Hampson explained that the singer should tilt the bottom of his pelvic cage slightly forward, unlock his knees, and then gently engage the muscles of his lower body. Those muscles, then, did all the work of holding the singer upright, and the chest, back and stomach muscles could be devoted to singing.

As I pondered these images, gradually light bulbs began to turn on for me. I realised that even though I might be turning my lower body through as I swung my golf club, in fact the swing was being led by my upper body, mainly by my arms and shoulders. My poor back was being dragged through the swing by the force of my arms, without any corresponding support from the muscle group below. No wonder it kept protesting.

Suddenly I understood what was required. I needed to apply to my golf swing the lessons learned from Thomas Hampson and those Yankee batters. My resulting technique goes like this:

When settling into my stance, I engage to the fullest the big muscles in my lower body, clenching those cheeks and bending at the hips. I also bend my knees with conviction. My lower body is now not only stabilised, it is also packed with pent-up energy.

Then I let my upper body swing free—not fast, not slow either, but free. On the backswing I *reach* out with my arms, extending them to the fullest degree, and continue the trajectory until the club hits me in the back. This is completely unorthodox, I know that, but the club bouncing off my back is my signal to begin the downswing. For me it's a key element in establishing a consistent and natural rhythm, and without it I get distracted thinking about just how far back to go!

When I am ready to reverse direction, I start by throwing my arms outward so as to get the same complete extension of the arms on the way back down. The full engagement of my lower body muscles permits me to push off with my back foot, propelling my weight forward and my hips around and thereby contributing all that pent-up energy to the power of the swing.

And there you have it. The fruits of a ten-year struggle to find a swing that—most of the time—works for me. I can absolutely guarantee that this will be of no use to you. You will have to figure out your own secret answers. At some stage, every golfer has to put aside lessons and take owner-ship of her own golf swing. That doesn't mean that lessons won't always play a role in your golfing life; they will and should. But the struggle to play well will only bear real fruit when you have sifted through all you have learned and fig-ured out what makes sense to your body and your way of feeling the movement.

Anybody reading this who *is* naturally athletic will prob-ably be thinking, 'Duh, that is so obvious.' Obvious it may be to you, but not to those of us who never even learned to throw a ball properly when we were children (and still can't). The problem is twofold. If it comes naturally to you, you are usually incapable of explaining it to an athletic dummy. Also, you can get the necessary power without having to bend your knees to a forty-five degree angle and squeeze your bum like you've got the runs. You can get more from less, and those of us watching you simply cannot tell just what it is you are doing. My husband is not a tall or powerfully built man, but when he is on his game he can out-drive everybody in the field. What exactly is he doing with his knees, his legs, his hands? I can't figure it out and neither can he!

So if you have reached a plateau in your golf game or, worse, are backsliding, think about Thomas Hampson singing Verdi, or your favourite athlete clenching his muscle-bound bum. It may not improve your game, but it's bound to improve your mood.

THE 9ᵀᴴ HOLE
A Leap of Faith

You can do all the clenching you want, but you'll never have a good golf swing if you don't also make a leap of faith. A good golf swing, indeed a good stroke in any sport, requires trust: trust that, having taken your backswing, your arms and the club will now complete the job without any further help from you. This is very, very difficult indeed for the non- athlete, even worse if you happen to be a control freak like I am.

The temptation is strong to try to control what the club head does, to guide it back to the ball, but that simply does not work. You lose all your power, but that's the least of it. You are likely also to either top the ball or smack your club head into the ground.

Instead what you have to do is what Miguel Sedeño, the wonderful pro at Valderrama, showed me one day. 'Throw the club at me,' he said. He was standing to my right, about four feet away from my shoulder. '*Cómo?*' I asked. I thought I had misunderstood his Spanish. Being an inveterate multi-tasker, I do my golf lessons in Spanish so I can learn two things at once. He repeated it and gave a brusque sweep of his hand towards himself. So I did my backswing and, with enormous trepidation and vivid visions of a visit to the emergency room at the local hospital, flung the head of my golf club at him. I finished the swing twisted in a knot and barely standing; the ball remained on the tee. *'Muy bien,'* he said. 'Do it again but this time don't forget to transfer your weight forward.'

I did it again and the result was spectacular. My ball sailed a million miles in a perfect arc and the swing felt so light I thought I'd hit a feather. I realised, too—and this was what Miguel was getting at—, that my arms had been extended as far as they could possibly go, like those of an Olympic hammer-thrower who swings his hammer round and round before releasing it. And as with his swing, the momentum of my arms and club had helped propel me through the golf swing. The sensation was one I had never felt before and it was exhilarating. Suddenly I understood that my arms are not supposed to guide the movement of the club; they are merely the means to connect the club to my body as the club head transcribes its arc.

How the club head managed to find its way back to the ball, I couldn't fathom. I still can't, and that's the whole point. That is why this part of the swing requires a leap of faith. You have to stop keeping your golf club on a short lead; you need to liberate it so it can find the arc that the laws of physics dictate for it and, amazingly, it works. It really is a miracle, and miracles require a leap of faith.

THE 10TH HOLE
Hot Wheels

If you want to know what golf is really all about, buy a little quiver golf bag or a very light one with double shoulder straps, put only half your clubs in it, and walk the golf course carrying your equipment.

There is no more liberating feeling than striding along the fairway completely self-sufficient, marching right up to the green without having to drag your trolley around the outside, and enjoying the sound of birdsong uninterrupted by the whine of an electric golf buggy. In other words, the best golf is golf with no wheels at all and in the winter when the ground is damp I often do it myself.

But as a practical matter, on most days golfers want to have handy their full set of clubs, their rain jacket and umbrella and an entire pocket of spare balls just in case. And others like to have mammoth, shiny leather golf bags just like the pros, bags that put your back out when you lift them, even empty. And so mankind invented electric buggies, caddies and trolleys.

There is a time and a place for golf buggies. In fact, there are days when playing without one can lead to hospitalization: when the sun is mercilessly hot or when the course is especially hilly. And for older people, using a golf buggy can prolong their golfing pleasure for years. But it isn't the same as walking.

When you use a buggy, you do only three things: you ride, you chat with your riding partner, and you hit the ball. And you diminish the great game of golf. For golf played on foot is a rich experience, offering a vital contact with mother earth. As you advance along the course, your view uninhibited by a buggy roof, you see the trees from different angles, sense the ground rising, falling or sloping away, gauge the distances, admire the imagination of the golf course designer, feel the wind direction, test the ground conditions. It is an experience that both adds to your appreciation of nature and contributes to your understanding of the course.

When you ride in a golf buggy, how well you score takes on too much importance. The only objective is to get your body and your ball to the hole as efficiently as possible, and no roses are smelled along the way. If you happen to be having an 'off' day with your golf, you've nothing to distract you from self-flagellation.

So walk whenever possible. If caddies are available, you might want to hire one. A good caddie is a treat, and they can be especially useful when you are playing a new course. Sadly, these days not all caddies are good. Even in Scotland where you usually get excellent caddies, you'll still get a loser once in a while. When we played St Andrews, my husband's caddie was nursing a serious hangover and I thought we were going to have to carry *him* around the course. And the one time I had the stupendous privilege of playing Cypress Point, the caddies wore blue jeans and dirty trainers and ate their onion-filled sandwiches on the tenth hole!

What's more, if you are playing in a four-ball and each person has a caddie, the group striding down the fairway resembles a small army and it takes a superhuman effort to maintain your concentration. Nevertheless, a caddie who can figure out your game quickly and tailor his advice accordingly, who can read the greens and find lost balls, is a gem.

So walk, and take a caddie if you don't want to carry your clubs. If there are no caddies, take a trolley. And the moment you reach the age when your body starts talking back, get an electric trolley. Nothing has done more to conserve my energy and spare my back than my splendid Hill Billy, which these days come in designer colours to match your every outfit.

On the whole, men think it is wimpish to use an electric trolley unless they are at least seventy years old. I don't understand this because they don't think it is wimpish to use a caddie, even when they are only thirty years old. Women, on the whole, are more practical and most of them figure out well before they are seventy that it makes sense to save their energy for hitting the ball, not dragging twenty-five pounds of golf equipment up and down hill for five miles. I recommend getting an electric trolley at the first twinge of the back, elbow, knee or whatever is your weakest link, or even if you just feel pretty tired when you come off the course.

Here is what I didn't realise about electric golf trolleys before I got my first one: that hauling clubs is only one of their many uses. Because an electric trolley carries on rolling without your help, they permit you to:

- Effect a change of wardrobe while walking between shots. This is very useful on the many days when the rain is stopping and starting and the sun is moving in and out of the clouds.
- Eat your lunch between shots (no onions please).
- Fix your hair when it is blowing in your face.
- Write down the scores from the previous hole.
- Check the Stroke Saver booklet in advance of your next shot.
- Cut off the hang nail that is bothering you.

- Get out some clean tissues and blow your nose.
- Rearrange the contents of your pockets because you just put on a jacket and now you can't reach into the pockets of your gilet.
- Put on sunscreen.
- Put on hand cream.
- Put on lipstick.

All of these things are very hard to do one-handed, which is what you have to do when the other hand is busy pulling a normal trolley.

So pick your wheels well, depending on the conditions on the day. But I urge you, if you have never once walked the course carrying your own little bag, try it. You might just like it.

THE 11ᵀᴴ HOLE
Big Girls Do Cry

A couple of years after I took up golf, in one of those all-too-brief intervals when my swing was working reasonably well, my husband and I spent a long weekend at a resort in Novo Sancti Petri on the Costa de Luz, near Cádiz in southern Spain.

Playa Barrosa, the beach in Novo Sancti Petri, is beautiful. The sand is white and deep and the beach stretches for miles, bordered by lovely, un-spoiled dunes. It is usually deserted—for good reason, for Playa Barrosa is also extremely windy. Less than fifty miles southeast stands Tarifa, only eight miles across the Straits of Gibraltar from North Africa, and the Atlantic winds regularly surpass force six as they channel through this narrow opening into the Mediterranean. Tarifa has a justly deserved reputation as a windsurfers' paradise, and the only people who brave the beach there are brawny hunks hefting their boards and their goose-fleshy girlfriends shivering behind wind shelters.

There was one golf course at that time in Novo Sancti Petri, and although it was no match for the beach in terms of beauty, neither was it exposed to the winds. Anyway, it was there and so we had to play it. As is usual when two people play a resort course, the caddie master teamed us up with another two players. Typically you end up with another couple and almost always they are enjoyable and courteous company. That day was no exception.

I acquitted myself decently on the first four holes, but on the fifth hole I shanked my drive deep into the pine trees that lined the fairway. It took me three shots to get my ball out from there and then I put it into a fairly benign greenside bunker from which I was utterly unable to extricate myself. I picked it up and bravely made my way to the next tee.

On the sixth hole I topped my drive and sent it skidding to the left into some water. It then took me five further shots to get near the green, whereupon I managed to send the ball shooting clear across it twice before I had any need of my putter.

By this time I was thoroughly tense, and any chance of achieving a smooth flowing swing was quite gone for the day. The other couple, who at first had been patient and sympathetic, began walking off the green before I had putted, knowing I had no chance of getting even close to the hole. I couldn't decide whether I was furious that they were assuming the worst, or happy that they were ignoring my humiliation.

Things didn't improve over the next few holes even though I tried every trick my pro had taught me about how to deal with a day such as this. I left my woods in the bag and stuck to my irons; I shortened my backswing; I teed the ball up on the fairway; I stopped my swing at the top of my backswing to make myself slow down; I even stopped it half way up the backswing to check the position of my hands and arms; I separated my two hands on the grip. Nothing worked.

In desperation I finally just picked up my ball and walked a few holes in an effort to calm myself down. This helped a little and I managed to limp along to the 18th hole and get my ball to within thirty yards of the green. The end was in sight. A little bump and run up to the green, two—or four—

putts and I could make a dash for the swimming pool. I took out my trusty lob wedge, played my shot and the ball sailed straight up in the air into a hovering pine tree and lodged itself cosily in the crook of a branch.

I grabbed my trolley and, looking neither left nor right, pulled it hard around the green and over to a wall bordering the course, sat down and began to cry. Not just cry, bawl. My husband came over and tried to console me but I was inconsolable. I sobbed and sobbed, my shoulders shaking with anguish, rage and frustration. It was easily ten minutes before I could pull myself together enough to stumble back to the hotel. On the way I managed a plaintive cry of self pity. 'I knew learning golf was going to be hard,' I moaned to my husband, 'but I didn't think it was going to be THIS hard.'

For me, there are still many times when golf proves to be THAT hard. At least once every six months I have a day when I feel completely humiliated. But I'm ready for it now, and the only time my game made me cry was in Cádiz.

THE 12ᵀᴴ HOLE
The Mother of All Bags

The other day I decided it was high time I cleaned out my golf bag. Here is what I found:

14 clubs, 6 with head covers
1 extendable 'fishing rod' for ball retrieval
1 umbrella
1 towel
3 membership tags (this year's, last year's and one from my previous club)
1 rain hat
1 winter woolly hat
1 pair rain pants
1 rain jacket
1 jumper
1 towelling scarf
1 pair winter over-gloves (bought at St Andrews on a July winter's day)
4 disposable hand warmers
1 plastic golf bag cover for rainy days
18 golf balls
Two dozen tees of various colours

17 plastic ball markers (for use on the green—handed out free at many clubs, hence the quantity)

11 golf gloves (at least half with holes or stiff with dried rain and sweat)

1 tiny brush for cleaning club heads

9 pitch mark repair tools (these are also handed out by many clubs in the fervent hope that you will tidy up after yourself)

8 small pencils (there are a further 35, at least, lying around at home)

1 elbow brace

1 small plastic bag containing a reeking and slimy banana peel

4 squashed cereal bars

3 empty wrappers from same

7 small packets of tissues

2 empty wrappers from same

A lot of litter (not mine, but picked up off the golf course—once a housewife, always a housewife)

1 empty plastic bag (awaiting the next banana peel)

1 small water bottle

1 tiny felt bag for safekeeping my gold watch when I forget to leave it at home

£23, 42 pence, $11 and €14

1 copy *Rules of Golf*

1 small spiral-bound plastic-paged *Quick Rules of Golf* (my bible)

7 plasters

4 hair grips

1 small bottle aspirin

5 loose aspirin (mostly pulverised)

1 spare towel ring

1 handicap card

1 shopping list

1 bottle sunscreen

1 scrap of paper with the phone number of my roofer

12 scorecards from various golf clubs (some used, some blank)

7 Stroke Saver books from various courses

1 top from a Lucozade bottle

1 set of keys to my golf locker

9 self-stick name labels for marking golf clubs (a very good idea for when you leave a golf club behind on the course)

3 torn green-fee tags from other clubs

You get the idea. Just like any woman's handbag, my golf bag is full of a multitude of useful, just-in-case items. (The used banana peel I keep in case I want to tell some man to go slip on one when he is giving me unsolicited advice.)

But don't get the idea that there is anything chaotic about my golf bag. On the contrary I know exactly—I mean *exactly*—where everything is. A golf bag is really the ultimate handbag, with different sizes and shapes of pockets for all types of items.

So when it comes to buying a golf bag, it is best to choose it yourself. You'll want to get one that fits your own personality and system of housekeeping, and then distribute your belongings in a way that makes sense to you. This really is important. The logistics of preparing for and playing a round of golf are daunting unless you are pretty organised. Let's say you're two couples on holiday and playing a new course. It usually goes something like this:

After arguing about how early to leave for the course, your husband wins and you leave later but, since he didn't allow time for getting lost and you did get lost, you arrive at the course only five minutes before your allotted tee time. Whereupon one person discovers that he left his shoes at home and so will have to buy a pair, another goes to pay the green fee but realises that his credit card is in the car, but his wife has the car key and she is in the ladies locker room, which she in turn took nearly the whole five minutes to get into, because you need a code to get in and she had to go back and ask in the pro shop for the number. Another member of the group has to get her spikes changed because the course requires soft spikes and hers are metal.

Meanwhile the husbands are arguing over who is treating whom. You think you are ready to play, but realise you need one final trip to the ladies' room. The other husband has gone off to the practice green without telling anybody. Meanwhile trolleys have to be rented, extra balls bought. The women have just discovered that there are no guest lockers so they have to run back to the car to lock their handbags in the boot but now it is her husband who has the car key and he is the one on the practice green…and on it goes.

By the time you get to the tee you are panting and harassed, everybody is mad at everybody else, and then you realise that nobody picked up any scorecards. The caddie master is trying to explain that you are not allowed to take your trolleys between the green and the greenside bunkers, and although you are trying to listen politely it's hard because your husband is telling you to get down to the ladies tees.

In such a situation, if you cannot quickly find a decent ball and a tee, get a pitch mark repair tool into your pocket, your hand into a wearable glove, your driver out and your ready smile pasted onto your face in ten seconds flat, you are in serious trouble. Whereas if you are more organised than everybody else in the group you will have the time, while they are still rummaging and running around, to do a few warm-up exercises and stretches. You can even take a few practice swings while the men are driving and taking their inevitable 'mulligans' because, in the tension of the moment, they have both blasted their first shots right into the woods.

Golf is really a fun game, but you may need to remind yourself of that during moments like these. A well-equipped, well-organised golf bag can be your saving grace.

THE 13TH HOLE
Mulranny Memories

One summer my husband and I decided to try our hand at some of the beautiful golf courses in Ireland. We only had five days so we limited ourselves to the west of the country, north and south of Galway.

We are not so fanatical about our golf that we forget to look around us. In fact we usually alternate a day of sight-seeing with a day of golf. So, between taking in the views on the Sky Road, soaking up some stunning scenery around Ballynahinch Lake and the Twelve Bens, and dutifully study-ing peat bogs as if they contained some clue to the Irish character, we managed to play Ballyconneely and Lahinch, both courses built on dunes along the coast. Ballyconneely is an expansive, rugged and windswept course, whereas Lahinch appeals to the eye with its endless hummocks, hillocks and hollows, and is memorable for the 'Klondyke', a massive dune right in the middle of the 4th fairway.

On our third day my husband remembered that our friend, Denis, had a summer house in the neighbourhood, so we called him and left a message at his office. Within hours a lengthy fax arrived at our hotel, full of details of how to get to his house, where to find the gardener who could show us around, the name of a good restaurant in the nearby town and, of course, the name of and directions to his own golf club, only a nine-hole course but his favourite in all of Ireland. We followed Denis's instructions to the letter and so, after admiring his beautifully refurbished nineteenth century manor house located on its own peninsula and complete with a boathouse full of toys for boys and men, a tennis court and a football pitch, at 5.00 p.m. we found ourselves driving into Mulranny Golf Course, a few miles along the coast from Westport.

Given the splendours of Denis's summer estate, we expected something pretty posh. Posh it was not. Next to the dirt car park was a wooden shack which passed for the clubhouse and pro shop. The door was unlocked but nobody was home. A small sign on an army issue desk said, in handwritten upper case letters:

GREEN FEE £10
PLEASE PUT IN BOX
TROLLEY £2

The trolleys in question were standing outside the door.

We paid our fees and surveyed the course. The setting was indeed stunning. The course was laid out on undulating land sloping down to high shoreline cliffs. In the evening light the view of the ocean to the southwest was breathtaking. Suddenly I saw that something was wrong with this picture: there were cows peacefully grazing as far as the eye could see. 'But where is the course?' I asked my husband. 'These are grazing meadows.' Yet the first tee was there to the left and, although the scene had at first appeared deserted, we suddenly spied another couple in the middle distance, clearly playing golf.

In my twenties I had lived on a farm in Normandy. Normandy is big dairy country and cows are everywhere. We raised some of our own, too, so I knew what an investment they represented. The idea of driving my golf ball into the middle of the herd went against everything I had learned in my years there, but clearly that was what we were expected to do. So I adopted the approach I always adopt when I want to be sure to avoid hitting something or someone (like a greenkeeper). I aimed right for one of them. I missed, of course, and my ball bounced harmlessly on the fairway.

Well, actually, the fairway and the rough were pretty much indistinguishable. The cows had seen to that. So after punching our balls out of a few hoof prints, we made it to the green where we found to our wonder (but of course!) they were surrounded by low barbed wire fences with little gates on one side. These little cow-less sanctuaries were as challenging as any greens I've played: the grass was about as even and manicured as my own back lawn.

By this time, my husband and I were laughing and joking like schoolchildren on an outing. All the tension that I normally carry around the golf course, all that tiresome striving for perfection, dissolved into the light of early evening. As we collected our balls and let ourselves out of the green enclosure, I gazed around at the scene. There were the cliffs, untamed nature at her loveliest. Here were the fields that had been grazed for centuries and carried the scars of tough weather and thousands of hooves. And here we were, two little human beings, out for some exercise, fresh air and a friendly match, playing a game on the land just as we found it. No heavy earthmoving equipment had shaped these links, no special grasses, no tining or aerating, no fertilisers or expensive mowers.

In that moment I had an inkling of how golf began: as an enjoyable pastime played on the land just as mother nature made it. My memory of that day has been my companion ever since, and in my moments of deepest frustration on the course I only have to think of Mulranny to remember that golf is, after all, just a game.

THE 14ᵀᴴ HOLE
Playing Fast But Not Loose

The best golf is fast golf. There is nothing more tedious than playing behind slow players, except for playing with a slow player. One of my worst golf course experiences ever was playing with a guy (yes, a man) who not only could not decide what club to use, but when he did decide he could not find it in his bag.

Fast golf does not mean you should ever take your shot fast. Each shot counts and you have the absolute right to take your practice swing, take your stance, wiggle and waggle a little, look at your target a few times, and then take your shot.

But there is a lot you can do, both before playing and between shots, to speed the game along. If you are playing a new course, go first to the pro shop to check out a few things such as whether the distance measurements on the course, such as special stakes or marked on the sprinkler heads, are to the front or centre of the green. Buy a Stroke Saver book if they have one. A knowledgeable golfer is a fast golfer.

Make sure you pick up your own scorecard. Usually one of the men will appoint himself official scorekeeper, which is fine: one less thing for you to think about. But you'll need a card to find out the distance, par and index for each hole, as well as to see the Local Rules which will be printed on it.

If the course has no Stroke Saver book, look around you at each tee. Many courses have a little placard at the tee—the men's tee, natch—with a diagram of the hole. Take a minute to look at this while the men are teeing off, and plan your strategy.

While walking up to your ball (one of many very good reasons to walk the course rather than take a golf buggy), use the time to think about which club to use. Consider the layout of the hole, the position of the green, the obstacles and hazards, the lie of your ball as well as the distance to the hole and the wind direction and speed. If, when you reach your ball and it is your turn to play, you are still undecided about which club to use, take both out of your bag, bring them over to where your ball is lying, make a final assessment of the situation, toss the unused club between you and your trolley so you won't forget it, and then take your shot with complete conviction that you have chosen the right club.

If you do all of this preparation while you are walking between shots you will not only be ready, you will look ready. You will look like a serious sportswoman, one entitled to take her shots without distraction and pressure.

Here is a tiny tip that is always helpful to me: I always use a coloured ball if I am playing in a four-ball. That way I know which one is mine well before I reach it, and it gives me a little more time to think about my next shot.

Countries, golf clubs and players vary in their approach to walking the fairways. Some players like to adhere strictly to the rather militaristic approach, whereby everyone advances down the fairway in lock step formation, stopping at each player's ball in turn. In general, however, and especially here in the UK, players adopt a more practical approach whereby anyone whose ball is off to the side in the rough can advance ahead of the group—but keeping well to the side and staying aware always of what is happening behind—so as to have time to look for her ball and consider how to deal with it.

If your ball comes to rest under a staked tree, knowing the rules will help speed you on your way. If you have to ask somebody else what to do, you not only lose time, you present yourself as a golf dummy. Provided you are not in a competition, you should just set about retrieving and dropping your ball and when it comes time to announce your score at the end of the hole, explain that your score includes a penalty shot.[1]

When walking the fairway, don't amble along or start telling your life story. Walk purposefully to your ball. Conversation is fine, provided you and the other player are heading in the same direction and you keep up your pace.

There may be times when you can help another golfer who is in a spot of bother. For example, if your partner is holding up the group because she had some trouble in the bunker, offer to rake for her while she is taking her next shot, and don't hesitate to ask for that service yourself when you need it. Keep a keen eye on other players' shots so you can help them find their ball, another favour which you can expect in return.

One of the first things we learn when we take up golf is that the player whose ball is farthest from the hole is the one to play next. On many occasions it is not entirely clear whose ball is farthest away. It is not uncommon for two players to be rummaging around in their bag or taking a few practice swings, each assuming that it is the other person's turn. If in any doubt, simply ask the other player as you approach your balls, 'Is it your shot or mine?'

Sometimes golfers resort to what I call the 'ready-golf fallacy'. The idea is that, to save time, whoever is ready first

[1]If you are in a match or tournament, or playing a medal round, you must consult and get the agreement of your opponent or card marker before picking up your ball. (see Appendices A-C, The Rules of the Game)

plays first, even if her ball is closer to the hole. This system can help to speed up the game, but only if the players are good at communicating their intentions. Otherwise confusion reigns, and either two players play at the same time or play comes to a complete halt as the 'you go, no you go' comedy act takes over. One of the great advantages of standard golf protocol is that everybody knows exactly what she and each of the other players is supposed to be doing at any given time, which leaves them all free to concentrate on their shots. In ready-golf, this certainty is lost, confusion prevails and quite often the quality of golf drops.

When you are approaching the green, be sure to bring your trolley around to the side nearest the next hole. Apart from saving time, the walk around will give you a chance to read the green from all angles, which should improve your putt. In fact, if you've got time to do it before you play your approach shot, it increases your chances of getting 'up and down' in two strokes.

Around the green, communication is especially important. The rule of 'farthest from the hole' applies there too, but many players think that a ball off the green, even if closest to the flag, has priority over a ball that is on the green but farther away. This isn't true but, unless you are in competition, it doesn't really matter as you can agree amongst yourselves to alter the playing order. The point, as always, is simply to be clear with each other as to who is playing next. Communication! Do I need to say it again?

If you are playing a match, one great way to save time is not to putt at all if you can't contribute to winning the hole. Suppose, for example, that the other team is going to win the hole even if you sink your thirty-foot putt, or that your partner has already won the hole with her stellar birdie. Then just pick up your ball and move on to the next hole. If everybody does this, you can shorten your round time by maybe half an hour, and arrive that much sooner at the 19th hole.

One place where a lot of time can be lost is on the tee. This can happen when the hole is a par three and the player with the honour can't decide which club to use, or the temperature has dropped and she wants to put on her jumper. It most commonly happens, however, when she decides to write down the scores for the last hole before hitting her drive, and then isn't even sure what they are. (This is a cardinal sin. To avoid committing it, confirm the prior hole scores of your playing partners while walking to the next tee and, if it is your honour, take your drive before marking the card). The teeing ground, therefore, is a time when ready-golf really does help. If it's another player's honour but she's upside down in her golf bag looking for an unbroken tee, simply say 'shall I go ahead?' and march up onto the tee. She'll be relieved to have the breathing space.

Without a doubt, there is an enormous amount to think about in golf. When you are starting out, everything is new: the equipment, the protocol, the rules, the layout of the course, the strategy for any given hole, and then there are the personalities of the other players, the conditions on the day, the various systems of scoring, and all that is before you even start thinking about how to hit the ball.

Plus, in the early days you're more likely to be hitting your balls into and out of weird places, making them hard to find and harder to play, and in addition you will almost certainly be hitting more shots than the other golfers in your group, since yours are shorter and less accurate than theirs. Yet they are expecting you to keep up. At times it can be simply overwhelming.

If you are lucky, a kind fellow player will see what is happening and will help out, by tracking down your wayward ball, coaching you on the rule when your ball goes in the water, taking your trolley around the green for you, imparting a little course strategy to help get you out of trouble, and just generally telling you that everything is o.k. and that you can take your time on your next shot (and hopefully not telling you how to fix your swing). If the people you are with are not like that, don't play with them again until you are more familiar with everything and more comfortable with your own game. In time it truly will become second nature, as automatic as loading the dishwasher or doing the school run, and much, much more fun.

THE 15TH HOLE
Golf is Not a Boat

If I inherited my father's love for golf, my brother and older sister inherited his passion for sailing. My brother regularly charters a boat and sails the waters of Maine. He persuaded us to go with him once. But only once: in my view, if you've seen one Maine pine tree, you've seen them all.

During the cruise he casually mentioned that he really wanted to buy a boat. 'You must be kidding,' I expostulated. 'Don't you know how much they cost? It will bankrupt you.' Well, he still has not bought his boat, but if he did it would take him years to catch up to what it has cost my husband and me to play golf. The only thing that has cost us more was educating our three children. And even that...well, it depends on what you include.

Do I include, for example, all the costs of the physiotherapist visits, massages and cortisone shots that have been required to keep my body functioning relatively pain free? Well sure. After all if I were a lunching lady I wouldn't need all that remedial treatment, would I? And do I include the cost of buying and running the little apartment we bought in southern Spain where we go, almost exclusively, to play golf? Yes, certainly, if you are comparing it to buying a boat. What is a boat if not a moveable holiday home?

So in fact, if you do include the price of the apartment, then the capital cost of playing golf can certainly rival that of owning a boat, because once you've bought your four walls and your beds, you then have to join the golf club—or clubs—, and the joining fees of prestigious golf clubs are not for the faint-hearted.

Golf doesn't have to be expensive. There are plenty of public courses, many of them absolutely wonderful. But once the game is under your skin you tend to get golf course creep, and you want to join a better one, and then another one, and then you have to pay all the annual dues as well, and eat up the food levies. And you'll notice I haven't even talked about buying the equipment you need—or want—to help you play your best.

Fortunately, the most expensive golf courses have some sort of share ownership scheme, so when you die or become decrepit, at least you can sell your share at the current market rate and recoup some of your costs. So my most burning question, when I think about how we've spent our hard-earned money over the years, is this: which will turn out to be the better investment, financially? Our golf club memberships, or our children's education? Since our children are all somewhat late bloomers, at this point in time the golf club memberships look set to win.

THE 16ᵀᴴ HOLE
Oh, The Places You'll Go

I was sitting in Gatwick airport just past midnight on a
dreary February night having a glass of wine with Petty, a
new friend, and Penny, whom I'd just met the week before,
and a weedy golf pro by the name of Simon. We were waiting to take a charter flight to Paphos in Cyprus.

My presence in the airport had come about like this. One
day I got a phone call from a golfing friend, Jane. She asked
me if I was interested in going to Cyprus in two weeks time
to spend five days at a golf school. It was an amazing deal:
the flights, the hotel (including breakfast and dinner), a
shared rental car, the lessons and a round of golf a day were
all included for the low, low price of £375. I had taken up
golf quite recently and I had all the zeal of the newly con-
verted. The idea of spending five days on a sunlit Mediterranean isle working intensively on my new passion was too
good to be true. I was interested.

'Are you going?' I asked Jane. Well, no, she had commit-
ments that week, but she'd heard about it from a mutual
friend, Carol, and it seemed such an opportunity, *somebody*
should take advantage of it. 'Is Carol going?' Well, no,
because Carol wasn't that keen on golf, but Carol's friend

Penny was going. Penny had taken up golf about when I did and Carol was sure I would get on well with her. They were really hoping I could go because if Penny couldn't drum up a couple more people, the trip would be a loss-maker for the pro and it would have to be cancelled.

My antennae should have leapt to attention on hearing that remark, but I let it pass and began to think who else I could recruit. Maybe Petty, a friend of other friends, who was a keen golf beginner like me. Maybe she would want to go. Well she did, and we went, and Jane and Carol are still full of remorse at dropping us into it.

Simon, the pro, seemed a nice enough chap. Clearly Penny was one of his steady clients, for they had a certain rapport—not at all sexual, rather maternal and protective on Penny's part. As we drank our wine in the departure lounge he turned to me and asked where I had been taking golf lessons up to now. I told him the name of my golf school. 'Oh I know about those guys,' said Simon. 'Their methods were discredited years ago.' If I'd had any sense at all I would have gone home right then, because the result of his disparaging remark was to make me so self-conscious I couldn't hit a single decent shot for the next five days. This may explain why I will never, ever, go back to Cyprus.

After a ghastly, sleepless night in a cramped plane, we landed at Paphos airport and dragged ourselves to our hotel. If we had been still in our back-packing days, this Spartan three-star hotel on the main street would have seemed an undreamt-of luxury. After all, it provided soap, and sheets. But once you are used to four- and five-star hotels, the downgrade comes as a shock to the system, only bearable if the cultural attractions of the destination, or its beaches, more than compensate for the discomforts. Cultural attractions and beaches there were, but in the time available we wouldn't be able to do them justice.

I had the foresight to immediately swap my room on the main street for a quieter one in the back. Apparently these quieter (higher-priced) ones were not meant for our cut-rate group, but I caught the receptionist in a weak moment and was the envy of the rest of our group, who spent the next five nights sleepless in Cyprus.

We soon made our way to the golf course, and what a disappointment that was. It resembled a wasteland, with more sand, dirt and rocks than grass. The course was also studded with telephone poles, which the course committee at least had the grace to designate as immovable obstructions. However, there was no such thing as preferred lies and to this day my golf clubs bear the scars inflicted by the stony ground.

Simon's teaching style was of the 'just hit your shot naturally' school, a method which is worse than useless for those of us who wouldn't know 'natural' if it came up and hugged us. An afternoon practicing pitch shots sticks in my mind. The rough there was pretty scrappy, and you needed firmness to hit pitch shots out of it. 'Relax your hands,' was the mantra of our self-satisfied pro. 'Let the club head do the work.'

I am sure that if I had been Ernie Els, this might have both made sense and worked. But I'm not Ernie Els—or I certainly wouldn't have been in Cyprus with Simon—and so it made no sense and didn't work. My club head simply stopped once it hit the lumpy ground, the only dent being in my confidence, never high to begin with.

Our group, in addition to Petty and Penny and me, included three other women of a certain age. They were shapeless, serious, opinionated, stingy and cliquish. They too were regular clients of Simon's.

Helen, Estelle and Stella hadn't travelled much so when, on the first afternoon, we three 'P's' decided to go look at a nearby museum and then drive on to see a ruined monastery, they (the three 'L's') asked if they could tag along. Why not? So off we set, in tandem, we three in our rental car and they in theirs.

The particular museum was entirely second class. Nevertheless we gave it a good forty-five minutes, patted ourselves on the back for being so virtuous, and were ready to go. Not so the three L's. They spent another forty-five minutes studying every artefact in the museum before accepting to travel on.

At this point they informed us that they were low on petrol. 'Well, maybe we should go on our expedition without you,' said we. 'No, no,' said they. 'We don't know if we will manage to find our way around without you.' So instead of heading for the hills, we drove to the nearest village. No petrol. There we were directed to the next village. No petrol. Finally, we ended up in a town ten miles in the opposite direction of our intended ruin. Petrol there was, and the three L's tanked up.

So at last, a good hour and a half later than intended and ten miles the wrong way, we embarked on our trip inland, through the hills to an ancient monastery highly rated in the guide book. Conscientiously, we kept checking in the rear view mirror to be sure our frumpy friends were still with us. At one point we missed a turn. We stopped, turned around, and headed back, gesturing out the window that they, too, should turn around. But the three L's drove on past without slackening their speed, without a wave good-bye, without even an acknowledgement of our presence.

We leapt out and began to gesticulate and yell, to no avail. Off they drove, over the crest of the hill and gone. We waited, anxious. They had no map, they had no guide book, they had no clue. Finally, we gave up and went our own way. At dinner that night we asked them why they had driven off. 'We decided to go see something else,' they said. No apologies, no explanations, no thanks for the museum tour or the petrol detour. We were mystified, and very cross.

Every afternoon, we three P's drove someplace to see something. Petty only knew how to drive an automatic, so I tried to do all the driving, for good reason: on those occasions when Penny claimed the wheel, we flirted with death on a regular basis. She would pass on blind corners and travel at breakneck speed on bumpy, badly engineered roads. More than once we were forced to swerve violently to avoid an oncoming lorry.

One afternoon we roared through a small, narrow-streeted village just as the mothers and grandmothers were walking the children home from school. No victims I am happy to say. However, I took particular note of a man on a ladder fixing his roof on the other side of the road. His ladder stuck well out into the road, just before a sharp corner. On the return journey I screamed at Penny to slow down as we approached the village. 'Have some consideration for the people who live here, for God's sake,' I shouted. She was deaf to my entreaties.

As we approached the blind corner, I begged her to slow down, pleaded, was practically crying. Sure enough, we rounded the corner and there was the roof man, getting on with his work, blissfully unaware of his impending Chaplinesque misfortune. In the nick of time Penny swerved to avoid him, then roared on, completely un-chastened.

Before dinner the first night, Penny came round to us all and said 'Look, we have a choice. We can eat in the hotel, where the dinner is included but is pretty awful, or we can go out. But in that case we will all have to share the cost of Simon's dinner, otherwise he won't be able to come.' I vowed never to let my daughter marry a golf pro, and then Petty and I agreed. After all, that would be a nice gesture to start off the trip.

On the second night, Penny came around and said the same thing. Petty and I looked at each other quizzically, but agreed. On the third night, the three L's bowed out, and the three P's paid for Simon's dinner. On the last night, Petty and I rebelled. We refused to contribute, and the whole group fell apart. We all went our separate ways for dinner, but before we went out, Simon approached us, somewhat sheepishly, and said that we owed him a further £35 for the trip. 'Why?' I asked. 'I thought everything was included.' 'Well, it was, but I calculated the exchange rate wrong between Cypriot pounds and English pounds. I multiplied instead of dividing.'

I was furious but I paid, and so did Petty. Simon had no idea how lucky he was that we were feeling nice. In fact he was so completely oblivious to the impression he had made on us, that for the next three years he kept me on his mailing list, sending me brochures about unsurpassed opportunities to learn golf at his clinic in Somerset, where he moved when he could no longer afford to live near London. As if!

The first moral of the story is, don't try to make your living out of golf unless (1) you are actually good at it, or (2) you want to live your life as a charity case. The second moral of the story is you get what you pay for, so think twice before signing up for that bargain holiday.

Since that trip, I have never again laid eyes on Penny or any of the three L's. As for Petty, however, out of this trip grew a beautiful friendship. If she could put up with the conditions and the cast of characters I dropped her into in Cyprus and still keep her sense of humour, if she could put up with all that and still want to be with me, then I was onto someone special. She became one of my very favourite golfing pals, the enduring silver lining of our stormy trip to Cyprus.

The 17th Hole
Never Up, Never In!

Mashie, niblick, cleek, baffie, spoon, brassie. These wonderful names from the nineteenth century show that golfers have never been at a loss for imagination when it comes to naming the equipment. Still you might wonder what the foregoing have in common with Bazooka Automatic, Beast, Voodoo Daddy, Stimp, Redneck Airhead, Futura Phantom, Tess, Ug-le, Frog, Thelma, Louise, Detour, Pink Blossoms and Monster. Simple. All of them are golf clubs, and the second group are all putters that you can run right out and buy today.

But be careful, because before you make your purchase you need a PhD in golf esoterica and a working knowledge of golf acronymia. Otherwise what on earth are you to make of the labels on the putters which flaunt the superiority of their MOI, HCG, IVM or SRT? And even if I were to tell you that MOI means Moment of Inertia and HCG refers to High Centre of Gravity, that IVM stands for Inverted Mass Technology and SRT means Saturn Ring Technology, would you be any the wiser about how to choose your putter? This might make for gear-head heaven, but it's closer to hell for most of us.

And so the manufacturers of these space-age beauties resort to other, more readily accessible features to attract your eye and open your purse. The Frog putter, for example, looks just like a frog, which is great if you think that by kissing it you might get a prince. But I can't imagine any golfer, man, woman or child, who would buy a putter called a Detour. And what woman would willingly purchase a putter called an Airhead except for the fact that it has this really smart red aluminium hosel (go look it up) with matching grip and putter cover? But we should all be grateful to Lange golf, specialist in women's golf clubs, for bringing us the Thelma and Louise putters for those days when the only solution to our golf woes is to drive off a cliff.

I have spent many hours trolling the web trying to understand putter technology, but when a looming case of mouse-related repetitive stress injury in my right arm called a halt to the fun, the only thing I was really convinced I wanted to own was the 'No-Bend-O' pitch mark repair tool. This marvellous gadget, as its title clearly suggests, enables you to repair your pitch marks without leaning over. If only it would retie my shoes while it was down there. But buy the 'Ms. No-Bend-O' at your peril: it has pink accents on the grip and ferrule (and you'll just have to buy one to learn what a ferrule is).

The choices among putters are legion. You can opt for a mallet, a potato masher, a pipe, a T or a lateral line putter. You can ponder the benefits of single, double or multi-layered inserts, C groove or sole rudders, heel or centre shafts, plumber neck or flare tip blades and a wide range of materials from persimmon to lightweight aircraft-grade aluminium, plus at least twenty different systems of alignment. Don't underestimate the impact on your game of choosing correctly between rear-, front- or high-weighting, but if you haven't a clue, buy the Louisville Stimp which has a system of weights in the club face that you can adjust depending on the speed of the greens. Great! All we need is one more thing to think about or lose. Does the club come with spare screws?

All this choice and I haven't even mentioned those weird looking implements called broomstick putters or belly putters. What's perfectly clear is that the putt is a stroke that drives golfers crazy and the equipment manufacturers know a good thing when they see it. Go into your golf club pro shop or the nearest golf store and you can expect to find approximately four times as many putters to choose from as drivers. This is surprising when you consider that the million-mile drive is the greatest ego trip for most golfers. Obviously the putt, whether twenty feet or only two feet, is the source of the greatest anxiety the game has to offer.

There is really only one way to choose a putter that is right for you, and that is to try out a few. Choose the one that feels the most comfortable and natural when you take your putt, and which also just plain makes you feel happy when you take it out of your bag. If that means it also needs to be green, or pink or purple, or have a mahogany finish, well I say simply, 'Go Girl!' And once you have decided, go on-line to eBay or one of the many websites that sell discounted or second-hand golf equipment and you'll probably find it at half the price. Thanks to all those frustrated golf nuts out there who think the latest equipment will fix all their faults, there is a thriving market in used golf clubs of every make and model.

Sooner or later on the putting green you will hear some person, well, some man naturally, advise you not to leave your putt short. 'Never up, never in' is a fairly standard bromide which, to me, simply reveals a whole other category of anxieties common among males, and is better suited for a Viagra ad. I have missed just as many second putts from over-long first putts as from those I've left short. The only time it is really just plain stupid to leave your putt short is when there will *be no* second putt, for example if you're in a match and you'll lose the hole if you don't sink your first one.

If you've read any golf instructional books, you've no doubt read in all of them that the secret to winning in golf lies in the short game. I don't want to belabour the point but it's true. Get some lessons to learn the basics and then practice, practice, practice, and don't fret if your stroke looks different from everybody else's if it works for you. Putting is probably the most idiosyncratic stroke in the whole game of golf, and the wealth of available putters is proof of that.

Skill at putting (and chipping and pitching and short sand shots) will become even more important as we get older and start losing length. How many times have you played with another woman fifteen years older than you and the following happens, hole after hole after hole? You out-drive her by fifty yards. You hit a second shot with a positively orgasmic flight path but which ends in the greenside bunker. You get out a little sloppily and then three-putt for a six. She hits short but reliably straight shots and gets to within thirty yards of the green in three, already one shot over regulation. She then proceeds to pitch on to within eight feet of the pin and sink the putt to score a five. Over and over again she sinks putts from four, six, ten, even twelve feet, and her pitch and chip shots always put her within that range. You simply cannot beat her, especially if her handicap is higher and you have to give her strokes. It's completely maddening, mostly because we know in our hearts that we seldom practice our short game except for a few minutes before a match, and we have only ourselves to blame.

So if you are losing matches because of your putting, that doesn't mean it's time to throw away your Bazooka Automatic and buy a Voodoo Daddy. It just means it's time to go the practice ground and work on your short game. You might want to adopt the habit of writing on your scorecard not just your total number of shots for each hole, but also how many putts you took as well as how many shots from sixty feet out. If the former number isn't less than thirty for the whole round, go back to work on your putting, and if the latter is more than three for any hole, you need to brush up on your total short game.

Many people will tell you that there is nothing more thrilling than a killer drive right down the centre of the fairway. Those shots *are* wonderful, no doubt about it. But sinking a ten- or fifteen-foot putt to win the hole for your team can bring on sheer, fist-pumping, high-fiving delirium that is pretty hard to match.

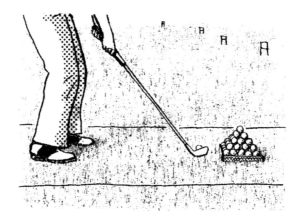

THE 18ᵀᴴ HOLE
Fear of Flailing

I may have taken ownership of my golf swing, such as it is, and of my body with its various frailties, but ownership of my own mind still eludes me. I am a classic case of the person who can nail her shots on the practice range, but mishits them on the course. Over the years my concentration has improved and I am less easily put off by outside distractions. I've narrowed my 'swing thoughts' to simply clenching my bum and throwing my club at Miguel. I know the feel of a really good golf swing and I can even do it sometimes. But only sometimes!

When I play golf with new people, I am generally quite nervous and consequently I play a pretty pedestrian, unremarkable game. But I always hit five or six shots that leave them gaping in astonishment. At the end of the round, after totting up my (usually) high score, one of them will say, 'With golf shots like I saw you hit today, your handicap is going to start dropping really soon.' I have been hearing this for ten years and my handicap still stands at twenty-five.

As I see it, I have a couple of problems to overcome. The first is that I have talked myself into believing that I am not a natural athlete. How many times have I said it in this book alone? Too many. That *is* my current self-image, but that doesn't make it true. I have good athletic DNA all around me; surely I got at least a gene or two. One of my New Year's Resolutions is to think about myself differently, to persuade my inner athlete to come out and flex her muscles. If I succeed, it will mean giving up my perennial excuse for bad golf. Am I ready for that?

Another hurdle is my 1950s 'good girl' training, which excelled at inculcating self-effacement. Good marks were expected but priding oneself on them was a sign of a swelled head. To be pushy meant being ugly, to be showy spelled slutty, to cause offence was inconsiderate and self absorption a deadly sin. The way that translates to the golf course defies belief: if I start to win, I dial back my desire for fear of offending. After receiving a compliment for a great shot, I fluff the next few just to prove that I'm not a threat. All this makes it difficult to play good golf.

Clearly I have a real conflict going on. I adore golf and I would love to play it better. I practice hard, I play often, I am committed. But walking up to my ball, taking my stance, I don't feel or act committed. I act careful.

I'm careful about my body, careful about the grass, careful about my equipment. When I hit a bad shot, it is not usually due to a faulty grip or to my hands turning over on the take-back, or even to not squaring up the club face at impact. It is usually because I don't do something *enough*. I don't shift my weight far enough onto my back foot on the backswing, or I don't turn my shoulders enough, or I don't lift my arms high enough or I don't cock my wrists enough. I hold back. I rein it in.

I know what it feels like to take a leap of faith, to throw out your arm and pray for a miracle. But one leap is not enough. You have to do it every time you take a shot, and that's pretty hard if your governing principle is carefulness.

I've read many of the golf self-help-your-head books. Some are so full of hot air they would float if you let go of them. Others have useful insights and suggestions to offer, and sometimes I think I'll have to go and hire a confidence coach (just in case I hadn't already spent enough on the game). And then I think that maybe my best coach is right here in my family: my son.

My son is a gorgeous athlete. He must have gotten a big helping of the family's good-athlete genes. He is tall, graceful, ambidextrous and fast. His coordination is superb and his instincts are excellent. He has desire and incredible tenacity, and he is utterly fearless. None of those words describes me, except for the part about desire and tenacity. I don't know anybody who has worked as hard at her golf as I have, with so little to show for it!

No amount of effort is going to make me taller, or ambidextrous, or graceful or fast. My coordination has improved as I have practiced, but there is nothing natural about it and my performance is totally learned, not instinctive. So as I see it, there is only one area left where I might make some strides, and that is in the fear factor.

It isn't just my golf. I am a careful skier and a careful tennis player. I have a lifetime's legacy of fear-filled sporting behaviour to overcome. But I know what it looks like to be committed, to be bold. My son is a champion double-black-diamond mogul snowboarder. When he catapults all six feet five inches of himself down the slope it is a wondrous sight to behold. No fear there. I remember a holiday when we played family tennis and he hadn't held a racquet in five years. During the first set he was all arms and legs, lunging here, flailing there, testing slices and slams, drop shots and volleys. Every ball went out and I beat him 6-0. By the second set he'd found his groove and all the same daring, edgy shots went in. I couldn't return a thing.

That is what I want to do on the golf course. I want to flail and lunge and throw myself into the swing with nary a thought for how I look, what my score will be or whether my drive ends up in the next county. I feel sure that if I dared to do that, I would find my groove eventually and then, finally and at long last, my handicap would drop.

I'm working on getting up the nerve. I'm pretty sure that the only thing standing between me and a much better game of golf is my fear of flailing.

Appendices

APPENDIX A
The Rules of the Game: I

At an early stage along your golf learning curve, when you are still struggling to make sense of the rules of the game, you will no doubt encounter examples of the following two types of women golfers. First, there are the rule bullies, who know (or think they know) every rule and every point of etiquette, and don't let you forget it. Try to avoid playing twice with a rule bully. And then there are those who talk about rules the way they talk about maths: that self-deprecating 'I never was any good at maths', or 'I never was able to understand maths', becomes 'I don't know anything about the rules' and 'the rules are so complicated, they make no sense to me.'

Incidentally, there is only one kind of male golfer: they all act like they know all the rules all the time. Some of the them actually do, and you can learn a lot from them. Others only think they do, but if a woman golfer knows the rules better than her male golfing companion, her superior knowledge is not usually welcome. Surprised?

My view of the rules is this: you do yourself a big disservice if you don't have a grasp of the basic rules as well as the remedies for the most common predicaments. It is good practice to carry in your bag the small booklet entitled *Rules of Golf* as approved by R&A Rules Limited and The United States Golf Association[1]. You can usually get this free from your golf club or else you can buy it from www.randa.org for the cost of the postage. If you don't

---

[1]R&A Rules Limited and The United States Golf Association. 2007. *Rules of Golf and the Rules of Amateur Status 2008-2011.* 31st Edition Effective 1 January 2008. All quotes in the Appendices, and the quote in The 3rd Hole, are from this Edition of *Rules of Golf.*

know the rules, you are in grave danger of cheating and in a competition you will be penalised. In addition you invariably hold up play while you get help sorting out your predicament. Furthermore, if you *do* know the rules, you are in a position to take advantage of the best option available to you whenever you are in a pickle.

The reason many of us get discouraged from learning the rules of golf is that they are written in the worst sort of legalese. The definitions are in one section, and each rule contains one or more cross references to other sections which are referred to by rule number. To find out the answer to any given question might take five minutes, include the consultation of four different parts of the rule book and require your strongest pair of reading glasses.

Here, as an example, is an excerpt from Rule 25-1c. Ball in Abnormal Ground Conditions Not Found, located on page 101 of *Rules of Golf 2008-2011* (all terms in special italics are defined in the Definitions section of the rulebook):

It is a question of fact whether a ball that has not been found after having been struck toward an *abnormal ground condition* is in such a condition. In order to apply this Rule, it must be known or virtually certain that the ball is in the *abnormal ground condition.* In the absence of such knowledge or certainty, the player must proceed under Rule 27-1.

If it is known or virtually certain that a ball that has not been found is in an *abnormal ground condition,* the player may take relief under this Rule. If he elects to do so, … [he] must proceed as follows:
(i) Through the Green: If the ball last crossed the outermost limits of the *abnormal ground condition* at a spot *through the green,* the player may *substitute* another ball, without penalty, and take relief as prescribed in Rule 25-1b(i)…

It's enough to give you a headache. And if you think *through the green* is an odd term (particularly as it doesn't even include the green), how about *rub of the green* (which also has nothing to do with the green), *outside agency* or *dormie*. For this reason, *Rules of Golf* won't do you much good unless you devote at least half an hour one day to familiarising yourself with its contents and layout. Take it next time you have an appointment with a doctor who always keeps you waiting. The rules of golf are actually very logical and involve several simple but fundamental concepts, and once you get the hang of them you can start to predict what they are likely to say.

Here is one of the most fundamental concepts of the game of golf:

FUNDAMENTAL CONCEPT A:

Once you place your ball on the tee and start your stroke, you aren't meant to touch or manually move your ball again until you get to the green, where you must mark it and pick it up if requested to do so by another player, and where it is in your interest to mark it, pick it up and clean it even if you haven't been asked.

There are, however, certain situations in which you are entitled or even obliged to move your ball with *no* penalty. You get a 'freebie'!

In this Appendix I'll explain freebies. There are other situations where you have the option of moving your ball but at the cost of one penalty stroke. I'll cover those in Appendix B.

Situations Entitling You to a Freebie

- You are *entitled* to a free drop if your ball comes to rest in, or your stance or swing are affected by, an *abnormal ground condition*, which includes:

- *casual water*, which is water that isn't meant to be there (i.e. it is not a designated *water hazard*— more about those in Appendix B). Included in *casual water* are areas that may appear dry but where the water starts oozing up around your shoes when you take your stance.
- *ground under repair*, or 'GUR', usually marked by blue stakes or a blue line around the area. You might find that a Local Rule declares it mandatory to move your ball from GUR.
- a hole made by a *burrowing animal* (cute!). This does not include holes dug by dogs so pray that Fido stays off the course.
- your ball is embedded (read 'plugged') in its own pitch mark in any 'closely mown area' (read 'fairway').

Abnormal ground conditions are covered by Rule 25.

⊙ You are also *entitled* to take a free drop if your stance, swing and/or ball are affected by an 'immovable' *obstruction*, which is to say anything artificial such as the artificial surfaces and sides of roads and paths, rubbish bins, or barriers. (An *obstruction* might also be 'movable', in which case you can go ahead and move it, even if it means lifting your ball first. Then drop the ball back as close as possible to where it was.) Note that a dirt path is not artificial and thus is not an *obstruction*, unless defined as one by a Local Rule. *Obstructions* are covered by Rule 24.

⊙ And you are *obliged* to take a free drop if your ball is involved with a 'young tree' or other 'environmentally sensitive area' as defined by a Local Rule. This refers to a situation when, if you were to take your shot, you would be likely to damage the tree or sensitive area during your swing. It does not apply if your ball, once you hit it, might hit another young tree on its trajectory—worse luck! Check your scorecard to find out if the course has any Local Rules of this sort.

Relief

The usual remedy for any of these conditions is to take 'relief'. This sounds too much like an aspirin to me, and I think of it more like the 'get-out-of-jail-free' card in Monopoly. Either way, whenever you are entitled to a free drop it goes like this:

You find the *nearest point of relief*, that is, the closest spot (but not nearer to the hole) to where your ball is lying such that, if your ball were lying in that new spot, the cause of the problem would no longer be an issue. Then you drop your ball (clean it first) with your arm held straight out at shoulder height *within* one club length of that *nearest point of relief*. You can't just toss your ball over onto the nice grass, and 'within' means 'within'. How many players have I seen who measure one club length and then drop the ball outside that limit, as if they had just defined the border of a quarantine zone and were not allowed to set foot in it.

The way to measure one club length is to lay your driver (the longest club of course) down on the ground with one end at the *nearest point of relief* and the other in whatever direction you want but not nearer the hole. Then put a tee in the ground at the end of your club to mark the distance and put the club back in your bag (so you won't forget it). The reason for putting down the tee is that if your dropped ball happened to hit your driver, you would have to start the process all over again.

There are some occasions when, even though you dropped the ball correctly, you get to drop it again. These include: if the ball rolls more than two club-lengths from where it first hit the ground, or if it rolls into a hazard or out of bounds, or back into the situation from which you are taking relief in the first place. If also on the second drop any one of these things should happen, at that point even the rule makers are ready to give up and will allow you to manually place the ball as close as possible to where it first hit the course when you dropped it.

More or less clear? I promise it will become second nature. The only tricky bit can be figuring out the *nearest point of relief* which, oddly, might not always be on the same side of the condition, tree or water nearest to which your ball is lying. This is because the *nearest point of relief* includes room for your stance, which means that it must be far enough away from the condition such that you can address the ball and take your swing (using the club you would use for the shot if the condition were not there— sorry, can't use your driver for measuring this time) and still not have wet feet or risk bashing the poor young tree. Check out Appendix F to see a sketch of how this might work.

There are slight variations to this whole business of relief if you are on the putting green or in a hazard. On the green you have a few additional options. You can place your ball instead of dropping it, and the *nearest point of relief* may in fact be off the green. Furthermore you are entitled to relief if the condition/obstruction is both on the green and in your *line of putt* (i.e. though it might not affect your ball and stance, it does lie on the path the ball will— hopefully—take). Some golf clubs have a Local Rule which also allows relief from an immovable *obstruction* if it lies within two club lengths of both the putting green and your ball. A typical situation would be when your ball is a few feet from the green and a sprinkler head lies between your ball and the hole.

On the other hand, if your ball is in a bunker you have fewer options. You can only drop your ball *within* the bunker (unless you are willing to incur a one-stroke penalty, in which case you can use the 'Imaginary-Line-Option' which will be explained in Appendix B).

And if your ball is in a *water hazard*, there's no getting out of jail free under any circumstances. You have to follow the rules for *water hazards* which are discussed in Appendix B.

Local Rules for Freebies

There are two additional situations in which you might be able to move your ball free, and they involve Local Rules dealing with 'preferred lies' (also known as 'winter rules') or with an 'embedded' ball *anywhere* on the course, not just on the fairways. These are cases in which the committee in charge of the course grants relief on a temporary basis, usually in winter, due to general adverse course conditions such as extreme wetness and/or mud. The normal remedy is to mark the location of your ball with a tee, lift and clean it, and replace it within six inches of its original position but not nearer the hole. Choose your spot carefully when you do this: the moment you let go of the ball in its new position it is considered to be *in play* and you can't touch it again. These Local Rules, since temporary, are not usually written on the scorecard but will be posted on the bulletin board. Check for them.

Appendix B
The Rules of the Game: II

In Appendix A, I explained when and how you're allowed to move your ball without incurring a penalty stroke. There are many other times in the game of golf when your ball comes to rest in an impossible position, in which case you do have the option of moving it, provided you are prepared to pay the price of a one-stroke penalty.

When you start to get the hang of when and how to exercise this option, you begin to understand that the founding fathers of golf were incredibly astute. For the price of a single penalty stroke you can extricate yourself from some truly dire situations, and by clever use of the rules you can minimise the damage done to your score.

Dire Situations Which Might Merit Relief

Here are some situations in which you might want to move your ball at the cost of one stroke:

- **When your ball is in a *water hazard*,** that is, if it is actually *in* the water (or is virtually certain to be but you can't see it) or it lies within the boundary of the hazard as defined by stakes or painted lines—yellow for a normal *water hazard* and red for a *lateral water hazard*. Keep in mind that you are not required to move your ball just because it is in the water hazard; you can play it where it lies, but in that case you are not allowed to let your club head touch the ground before you take your swing. *Water hazards* are covered by Rule 26.

- **When you consider your ball to be 'unplayable'.** When *I* consider *my* ball to be unplayable? I consider my ball to be unplayable most of the time! This is such an astonishingly wonderful rule that it is actually difficult to credit it. But this is what it says in Rule 28 of the *Rules of Golf*:

  > The player may deem his ball unplayable at any place on the course, except when the ball is in a *water hazard*. The player is the sole judge as to whether his ball is unplayable.

  Think about it. Your ball is nestled up against a tree—sadly not a 'young tree'—and you'll probably break your wrist on the tree trunk if you try to play it. So don't. Declare it unplayable. Or your ball has come to rest in waist-high rough. Or your ball has found the hole that Fido dug. I don't think I need to extend the list; we have all been in these sorts of situations. But of course what we usually do is try to be heroic. Three shots later we finally declare the ball unplayable and our score is unsalvageable. This is where course management comes in. These are the times when we can either use our heads or leave them in the car in the car park. Ladies, the rules of golf are there to help you. Use them!

Remedies for Dire Situations

If either of the above situations occurs, that is if your ball is in a *water hazard* or you declare it unplayable, under penalty of one stroke you can usually choose from one of three remedies:

- **Remedy One. The 'Two-Club-Lengths' option:** Drop a ball to within two club lengths—but not nearer the hole—from where your ball was lying (or in the case of a *lateral water hazard*, from where it crossed into the hazard). I hope you will note the justice of this: you are paying one stroke for the right to move your ball, so you get *two* club lengths, not just *one*. (Note that the 'two-club-lengths' option is *not* available in the case of a regular *water hazard* (yellow stakes), only a *lateral water hazard* (red stakes).)

◈ **Remedy Two. The 'Go-Back-to-Start' option:** Drop a ball as close as possible to where it lay before you hit the offending shot. If the offending shot was your tee shot, and you saw the ball splash into the water or sail deep into rough you know is horrendous, this is often your best option. After all, you get to tee the ball up, have an open shot at the fairway and can use your longest club. Don't even bother walking up to look for your ball; simply take another shot from the tee with a different ball. This is called a *substituted ball*, and the shot will be your third: your first shot plus one penalty make two shots so far (described in the rules as 'stroke and distance'). The original ball is 'deemed' *lost* but you are allowed to 'find' it if you can do so quickly.

Although not required, it's a good idea to tell your playing partners exactly what you are doing so they do not assume you are hitting a *provisional ball* (see 'Lost Balls' below).

And it is a *very* good idea, before taking your remedy shot, to step back from your ball, clear your head and take a practice swing. In fact if you are on the tee and other players have still to take their drives, the rules of golf require you to let them go first anyway. So often it happens that a player rushes into her remedy shot and hits a clone of the first one. That means that her *next* remedy shot is her fifth shot; she already has a bogey and she hasn't even left the tee!

⊚ **Remedy Three. The 'Imaginary-Line' option:** Drop a ball behind you as far back as you want on an imaginary straight line which intersects (sorry, math dummies) both your ball position—or where it crossed into the *water hazard* if that is where your ball was—and the hole. This is probably the most misunderstood rule in the game of golf. Even some very experienced players think that the imaginary line is the one that intersects your ball and the tee. No, no, the idea here is to always keep your eye on where you are going, not where you came from.

Implementing this remedy opens up some interesting situations, like when you find yourself dropping your ball on the fairway of the adjacent hole (perfectly legal), or instead of coming out sideways from the ball-grabbing bush that thwarted you (because two club lengths is not enough to make a difference), you take your ball way back behind said bush to a more benign part of the rough. Don't ever forget that you can take the ball back as far as you want as long as you keep on the imaginary line. Do you begin to see how knowing the rules can open up your options?

Lost Balls and Balls Out of Bounds

There is another group of rules worth mentioning here, since the remedy is similar, and that is Rule 27 concerning a *ball lost* or *out of bounds*. A ball is declared *lost* if it cannot be found within five minutes. *Out of bounds*, or 'OB', is usually either delineated by white stakes or lines, or described in a Local Rule printed on the scorecard.

If your ball is *lost* or *out of bounds*, the only remedy available is the Go-Back-to-Start option: drop another ball back where your original ball lay before you hit the offending shot.

The high priests of golf have instituted a very practical, time-saving solution called the *provisional ball*. The idea is that if you *think* the ball you just hit might be *lost*, OB or in a *water hazard*, you hit a second ball from the same place, first announcing very clearly that it *is* a *provisional ball* (otherwise it will automatically be considered a *substituted ball*—see Remedy Two above). Then if, when you walk forward, you discover that your ball really *is* OB or you cannot find it, you don't have to sprint back to the tee, irritate the golfers following you, get all hot and sweaty and no doubt bungle your next shot too. You simply keep playing with the new ball. Your score at that point is the sum of the strokes played with both balls, plus one penalty stroke.

The rules stipulate that you continue to hit the *provisional ball* only until it is level with where you think the original ball is. If you then find the original ball you *must* play that one. Some of the saddest moments in golf are when your provisional shot is the most spectacular, straight-from-the-textbook shot of your golfing career, 210 yards straight down the fairway, and then you find your original ball in knee-high rough behind a tree and nestled against a large clump of dirt. I regret to say that at that point you are stuck with your original ball and, although you *can* decide to declare it unplayable, you cannot—no alas, you *cannot*—carry on with the *provisional ball*. You can elect the Go-Back-to-Start option, but then you must go back to where you hit the original shot and pray for another corker—which you almost never get.

Here is something else you cannot do: hit said spectacular textbook shot and then proceed to look only very half-heartedly and in patently the wrong place for your original ball. The good news is that you and your partner only have to look for five minutes and then you are allowed to declare it *lost*.

This might be the moment to draw your attention to Section 1 of *Rules of Golf,* the section on Etiquette and Behaviour on the Course. Here is a verbatim quote from the paragraph entitled 'The Spirit of the Game'.

> The game relies on the integrity of the individual to show consideration for other players and to abide by the Rules. All players should conduct themselves in a disciplined manner, demonstrating courtesy and sportsmanship at all times, irrespective of how competitive they might be. This is the spirit of the game of golf.

There you have it. If you find yourself playing with people who use a supposed lack of knowledge of the rules of golf, or the fact that your back is turned, to cheat, then my best advice is not to play with them again. In fact, since golfers usually play as they live, you might want to reconsider the friendship!

APPENDIX C
The Rules of the Game: III

In Appendix A, I set out the *most* fundamental of the fundamental concepts of the game of golf. Here is another one, verbatim from Rule 1 of *Rules of Golf*, paragraph 1-2. Exerting Influence on Ball.

FUNDAMENTAL CONCEPT B:

A player or *caddie* must not take any action to influence the position or the movement of a ball except in accordance with the *Rules*.

There are lots of ways in which a player might unfairly influence the movement of her ball, and which are therefore forbidden by the rules of golf. Here are some examples:

◉ **A player must not improve the position or lie of her ball**, the area of her intended stance or swing, her line of play, or the area in which she is to drop or place her ball. This means that you cannot remove, bend or break anything which is growing or fixed, other than in fairly taking your stance and taking your stroke. Neither can you eliminate an irregularity in the ground surface, or remove or press down divots, sand, loose soil or water. However, you may remove loose sand from a putting green and you may also repair an irregularity on the teeing ground. (Penalty for breach of these rules: Match Play – Loss of Hole; Stroke Play – 2 strokes) (Rule 13. Ball Played as it Lies)

THE VIEW FROM THE LADIES TEES

- **A player may not test the condition of a *hazard*.** This includes touching the *hazard* with her hand or club, or removing from it any *loose impediments* such as stones, leaves or other natural objects. Note that some clubs have a Local Rule permitting removal of stones from bunkers for reasons of safety, so check the scorecard. (Penalty for breach: Match Play – Loss of Hole; Stroke Play – 2 strokes) (Rule 13-4. Ball in Hazard; Prohibited Actions)

- **A player may not test the condition of the *putting green*,** by rubbing her hand over it or rolling a ball across it. In fact, she may not even touch the *line of putt* except to repair new or old pitch marks only (not spike marks or other damage), to remove *loose impediments* or sand, or while lifting her ball, placing the ball marker or measuring. (Penalty for breach: Match Play – Loss of Hole; Stroke Play – 2 strokes) (Rule 16. The Putting Green)

- Players *are* allowed to remove *loose impediments* from around their balls provided they are *not* in a hazard, but Beware! **If you cause your ball to move** when doing so, you will incur a one-stroke penalty and the ball *must* be replaced. Whenever I am trying to remove pine needles from around my ball, I am reminded of endless childhood games of 'pick-up-sticks', but my manual dexterity was much better then. (Rule 18. Ball At Rest Moved)

- A player's partner and/or caddie **must not touch the green while indicating a line for putting**, nor place any marker to indicate the line. (Penalty for breach: Match Play – Loss of Hole; Stroke Play – 2 strokes) (Rule 8-2. Indicating Line of Play)

When you think about it, these rules all make pretty good sense. In fact, if you didn't know them, you probably could have guessed them. If in doubt, just keep in mind the fundamental concept that you cannot take any action to influence the position or movement of the ball, except in accordance with the Rules. In other words, if you can't think of a specific rule that allows you to touch or move your ball, or touch the line of play, then the answer probably is that you can't.

APPENDIX D
No No's and Rule Riddles

There are lots of things we might do on the golf course which seem like perfectly rational things to do, but which in fact cost us penalty strokes. There are other things which we might neglect to do because they don't seem especially important, with the same result.

It's pretty depressing to incur completely avoidable penalty strokes when after all we get quite enough of them due to wayward shots. However, because in friendly games players often ignore these rules, it is easy to get into the habit of forgetting about them, only to lose a competition for an unnecessary mistake.

Silly Ways to Incur a Two-Stroke Penalty

The following are some of the most obvious ways you can inadvertently incur a two-stroke penalty if you are in stroke play or (except where otherwise indicated) the loss of the hole in match play:

- **If you ask for advice** from, or give advice to, anyone other than your partner, your caddie or your partner's caddie. Asking an opponent what club she used for a given shot, before you have taken yours, constitutes asking advice so resist the temptation to do that. Keep this in mind the next time you receive unsolicited advice!

  Matters of fact, such as the distance to the next green, or whether there are any hidden bunkers ahead, do not constitute advice so ask away about those sorts of things. It is also o.k. to ask any other player about the *line of play*—i.e. the direction of the hole—*except* on the putting green, where you can only ask your own team. (Rule 8. Advice; Indicating Line of Play)

◦ **If you play the *wrong ball*.** So make sure you know what kind of ball you are playing with and that it is a different brand or number from the balls of other players. You should even mark it in some distinctive way. Once you realise you have played the *wrong ball*, you have to go back and play the correct ball and if you fail to do that before starting the next hole, you are disqualified. So unless you are having a miserable day and seeking an instant exit strategy, it's best to play the correct ball the first time. (Rule 15. Substituted Ball; Wrong Ball)

If you can't identify your ball because the marks are hidden, you may lift it to identify it, but first tell your playing partners and don't clean it more than necessary to see the identifying marks. Then replace it back where it was. (Rule 12-2. Identifying Ball)

◦ **If your putt hits another ball on the *putting green*.** (Rule 19-5) The other person's ball is put back where it was (Rule 18-5) but yours must stay wherever it ends up. (This infraction carries no penalty in match play.)

◦ **If your ball strikes the flagstick** (whether or not attended, whether or not in the hole) or any person attending it, provided your ball was struck from on the putting green. (Rule 17. The Flagstick)

⊚ **If you play your tee shot from outside the *teeing ground*.** In addition, you have to take your shot over again. (There is no penalty in match play, but your opponent may require you to play a new ball from the correct place.) You are allowed to take your *stance* outside the *teeing ground*, which by the way extends backwards from the markers for two club-lengths but not one eyelash forwards. Use those two club-lengths to find a level spot to play from. (Rule 11. Teeing Ground)

⊚ **If you take a practice *stroke* during a round** (practice *swings* are fine), except that between playing two holes the player may practice putting or chipping on or near the putting green just played or the teeing ground of the next hole, provided that she does not unduly delay play. (Rule 7. Practice)

Other Avoidable No No's

Some infractions incur only a one-stroke penalty, for example:

⊚ **If you strike the ball twice in a single stroke.** You count the original stroke, of course, and then add one penalty stroke for the second strike. (Rule 14–4. Striking The Ball)

⊚ **If your ball hits your equipment** or that of your partner, and this includes your golf buggy. So take care where you park your wheels. You will also incur the penalty if your own ball hits *you*, your partner or either caddie, which is not the only reason you might wish to avoid doing that! (Rule 19. Ball in Motion Deflected or Stopped; paragraph 19-2)

- **If you carry more than fourteen clubs in your bag**. For this infraction of the rules you will receive the following draconian penalty for every hole played with the offending extra club: in stroke play, a two-stroke penalty up to a maximum of four strokes, and in match play, the loss of a hole up to a maximum of two holes. Painful!

  If you discover in the middle of the round that you have more than fourteen clubs, immediately declare the excess clubs to be 'out of play' and don't use them again. It is a good idea to put them upside down in your bag to avoid error. If, by the way, you borrow a club from your partner when you already have fourteen in your bag, that counts as having an extra club and results in the penalty. (Rule 4-4. Maximum of Fourteen Clubs)

On the other hand, you will actually be disqualified:

- **If you mistreat your scorecard**, for example by recording a handicap higher than actual or forgetting to record it all, or for neglecting to sign the card or getting your marker to sign it. There is no place for sloppy paperwork in golf! (Rule 6. The Player)

- **If you ignore any *Rule* or waive any penalty**. The fact that this is Rule 1-3, appearing on page 1 of The Rules of Play, might give you an idea of the importance the golfing powers put on this rule. So during a competition you do nobody any favours if you offer to ignore your opponent's infraction, as you will both be disqualified. When you are playing for real, it's best to opt for tough love.

Let it Rest

If your ball is at rest and it moves, the remedy and punishment depend on the circumstances. Generally speaking, if your ball was moved by an *outside agency* (see definition below) or by your opponent, her caddie or her equipment, or by a ball in motion, you incur no penalty (although your opponent might). Also if your ball has come to rest against a rake in a bunker, there is no penalty if the ball moves when you remove the rake.

However if you, your partner or either of your caddies has any role in moving it, or even *touches* it, you will incur a one-stroke penalty. Furthermore, once you have *addressed the ball* (defined as 'taken [your] stance and also grounded [your] club'), any movement of the ball thereafter is deemed to have been caused by you even if in fact it wasn't, and therefore you incur a one-stroke penalty.

As usual there are a few exceptions, most of them common sense. For example, you can touch your ball with your club head while in the act of addressing it as long as it doesn't actually move, and, believe it or not, it's o.k. if the ball oscillates as long as it ends up back in the exact same place! Also there is no penalty for knocking your ball off the tee in the act of addressing it on the *teeing ground*, because even though it has obviously moved, that ball is not yet *in play*. (Rule 11. Teeing Ground). Finally, there is no penalty if you accidentally move your ball while searching for it in an *obstruction*, or under *loose impediments* in a *hazard*, or while doing something legal like measuring, marking it or lifting it in accordance with a *Rule*.

However, *regardless of what caused the ball to move and whatever the circumstances,* a ball at rest that has moved or has been moved *must* always be replaced, unless it moves after you have begun your backswing and you complete the stroke. Failure to replace the ball results in a two-stroke penalty, making a bad situation even worse.

What does this mean, in practice? It means that if as you address your ball you accidentally tap it and it jiggles, as long as it returns to the original spot you haven't incurred a penalty. That's the good news. If, on the other hand, you are preparing to hit a ball which is resting precariously on top of some long grass, and it suddenly slides down into it, you have got to put it back up there. Good luck! Furthermore, if you are *responsible* for making it fall, or even if you are *not* responsible but you have already *addressed the ball* when it happens, then you incur a penalty as well.

One strategy worth adopting is to avoid grounding your club in tricky situations like this to minimise the chances of getting a penalty. It also pays to be extra careful in approaching the ball and taking your stance and backswing, so as not to disturb the grass and cause the ball to move. Easier said than done, of course, but that excuse won't save you from receiving the penalty. (The above is mostly covered by either Rule 18. Ball at Rest Moved, or Rule 12-1. Searching for Ball; Seeing Ball)

Golf Gobbledygook

The language of golf is charming but sometimes incomprehensible. Some wonderful terms are no longer relevant in golf but have made their way into general usage. For example the word 'stymie', which means 'a difficult or frustrating situation' or, as a verb, to 'obstruct' or 'thwart' according to the *Shorter Oxford English Dictionary* (2007), was originally used in golf to refer to the situation on a putting green when the ball nearer the hole lay in the line of play of another ball. As golf was originally played in Scotland, the owner of the farther ball could not require the owner of the nearer ball to mark and lift it, and therefore he had to find a way to play his shot around or over his opponent's. Such a player was well and truly 'stymied'.

Luckily many other colourful terms remain to enchant and mystify us. For example:

An *Outside Agency*, while it sounds vaguely like somebody's secret service, is simply anything which is not part of the match or, in stroke play, not part of the competitor's side. Examples of *outside agencies* include animals, spectators, referees, lawn mowers, tool sheds, signs and any other such things.

Rub of the Green is a defined term in *Rules of Golf* which basically means, 'tough luck, mate'. It is a *rub of the green* when your ball in motion is accidentally deflected or stopped by an *outside agency*. There is no penalty but you have to play the ball as it lies.

Through the Green means pretty much everything *except* the putting green. In fact it includes the whole area of the golf course except the *putting green* and the *teeing ground* of the hole being played, and includes all the *hazards* on the course.

Dormie, which if you understand French you might think means that you've fallen asleep, is a term used in match play to refer to the player or partners who are ahead by as many holes as there are left to play. The other side cannot therefore win, they can only lose or tie. So it is no time to be falling asleep.

Casual Water is not the opposite of 'tense water'. Rather it is the opposite of intentional water such as that found in a water hazard, and is defined as any 'temporary accumulation' of water on the course. There are some very fine points to note here, but they will not be included in the final examination. Snow and natural ice are either *casual water* or *loose impediments* at the player's discretion, which means you can either move your ball or move the snow or ice, whichever works best for you. Dew and frost on the other hand are *nei-*

ther casual water nor loose impediments so you can't move anything. Worse luck. And manufactured ice is an *obstruction*, either movable or immovable depending, I guess, on how strong you are. What manufactured ice would be doing on the golf course I can't begin to imagine, unless you hit your approach shot on the 18th hole into the cooler of celebratory champagne.

Timing is Everything

You only have five minutes to look for your ball until you have to declare it *lost*. Sometimes this is a blessing, like when you know your ball must be lying under some prickly, four-foot high nettles, whereas your *provisional ball* is a shot worthy of Annika Sorenstam. (From Definition of *lost ball*)

You're only allowed to wait ten seconds, counting from when you have walked up to the hole, to see if your ball which is poised on the rim of the hole is going to fall in. Sorry, it's not cricket to blow on it or stamp the ground next to it to help it topple over. (Rule 16-2. Ball Overhanging Hole)

Information Overload

There is a lot of information in these first four appendices. I have tried to present the most important rules in a way that helps make them logical and therefore more easily remembered. But you won't remember all of them all the time, and you won't find many amateur golfers who do. I suggest reading these appendices a few times to get the drift, and then try to get your hands on a copy of *Quick Series Guide to Golf Rules*. This booklet is a fabulous little spiral bound, plastic-paged summary of the main rules, organised by type of problem and containing useful diagrams. It is the best place I know to get a quick and accurate answer then and there on

the golf course. It is published by Luxart Communications
and can sometimes be found on www.amazon.co.uk. In addition, R&A Rules Limited have added their own Quick Rules
section in the front of the new edition of *Rules of Golf.*

APPENDIX E
Helpful Hints to Husbands

The following are verbatim quotes from *Rules of Golf*, Section I-Etiquette; Behaviour on the Course:

> This section provides guidelines on the manner in which the game of golf should be played. If they are followed, all players will gain maximum enjoyment from the game. The overriding principle is that consideration should be shown to others on the course at all times. ('Introduction')

> All players should conduct themselves in a disciplined manner, demonstrating courtesy and sportsmanship at all times, irrespective of how competitive they may be. This is the spirit of the game of golf. ('The Spirit of the Game')

> Players should always show consideration for other players on the course and should not disturb their play by moving, talking or making unnecessary noise. ('Consideration for Other Players')

> Players should not stand close to or directly behind the ball, or directly behind the hole, when a player is about to play. ('Consideration for Other Players')

> Players should remain on or close to the putting green until all other players in the group have holed out. ('Consideration for Other Players')

> It is the group's responsibility to keep up with the group in front. If it loses a clear hole and it is delaying the group

behind, it should invite the group behind to play through, irrespective of the number of players in that group. ('Pace of Play')

Players should avoid causing damage to the course by … hitting the head of a club into the ground, whether in anger or for any other reason. ('Care of the Course')

APPENDIX F
Diagrams for the Dedicated

Fix That Pitch Mark

Whenever you pitch your ball up towards the hole and it bounces on the green before rolling to a stop, check to see whether your ball has made a pitch mark, in which case repair it before leaving the green.

To do this, stick your pitch mark repair tool into the ground at a 45-degree angle just beyond the edge of the indentation and push it *gently* towards the centre of it. Do the same thing over and over again, each time inserting your repair tool a little further along in a circle around the indentation. Then tamp the area down with your putter head. If the area is not smooth, do it all again. Do not do, as I did at first, stick your repair tool in at an angle and try to lift up the soil under the indentation. Logical though it might seem, it in fact breaks the roots of the grass.

When is the job done? When you would be happy to putt over that spot!

Diagram of Relief

As mentioned in Appendix A concerning 'Relief', there are situations in which the *nearest point of relief* may not be on the same side of the tree, *casual water* or *ground under repair* as where your ball has come to rest. An example, using a young (staked) tree, is shown opposite. Although the ball came to rest on the right side of the tree, if the player were to take her stance on that side of the tree (Stance B), including allowing room for her backswing, the *nearest point of relief* (Distance B) would be farther away from where the ball originally came to rest than if she took her stance on the left side of the tree (Stance and Distance A).

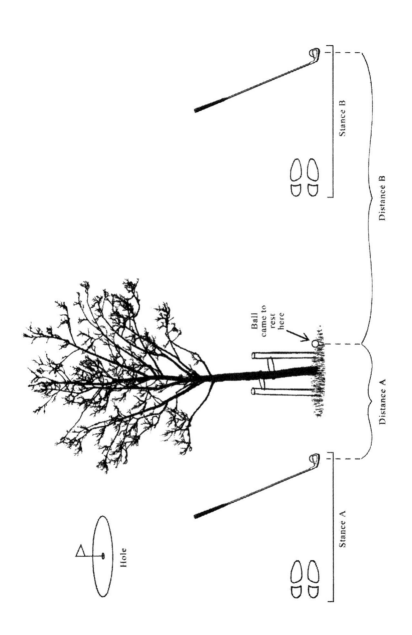

ACKNOWLEDGEMENTS

Many are the people who have patiently shepherded me along the path of learning golf. Dave Wilkinson of Knightsbridge Golf School trained me in the fundamentals of the golf swing and encouraged me in my darkest hours. Tom Wischmeyer, now at the Stadium Golf Center in San Diego, not only taught me the basics of the short game but pretty much everything I know about course management. Miguel Sedeño at Valderrama Golf Club explained to me the meaning of '*soltar*', both the word and the feeling, and I think of him as I try to 'let it rip' every time I take a swing.

Very special thanks to my best golfing pals: Sue Clifford, Petty Taylor, Kate Yates, Margaret Walker, Joan O'Neil and Rosemary Stockton. On good days and bad they have always been supportive, and are the best company in the world. Several of them also read the manuscript and gave me excellent suggestions for improvement, as did Debbie Cutfield, Judith Foy, Val Urquhart and Sue Deller.

The people who have laboured hard to keep my body together include Shirin Elling at the Earth Spa, Carsten Uth at Physiotherapy in Chelsea, osteopaths David Propert and Gerry Gajadharsingh at Health Equation, and Chris McLean of the Marylebone Physiotherapy and Sports Medicine Clinic. My wonderful rheumatologist, Dr. Cathy Speed, solved several hitherto intractable problems.

Big thanks to Anne and Bill Kneisel, our hosts in Lech where I wrote most of this book. Also to Bruce and Rose Nelan who read the first draft and pointed me in the right direction, and to George Feifer for believing in me for no especially good reason.

Thanks most of all to my darling husband, Ian, who right from the start believed I could do this and kept telling me so.